Seashore
Northern & Central California

Lurid Rocksnail

Seashore

Northern
& Central
California

Written and illustrated by
Ian Sheldon

The Publisher: Lone Pine Publishing

1901 Raymond Ave. SW, Suite C
Renton, WA 98055
USA

206, 10426 – 81 Ave.
Edmonton, AB T6E 1X5
Canada

202A, 1110 Seymour St.
Vancouver, BC V6B 3N3
Canada

Lone Pine Publishing website:
http://www.lonepinepublishing.com

Canadian Cataloguing in Publication Data

Sheldon, Ian
    Seashore of Northern and Central California

    ISBN 1-55105-144-3
    1. Seashore biology—California, Northern and Central.
    I. Title.
QH95.7.S436 1999   591.7699'09794'1   C99-910323-7

Editorial Director: Nancy Foulds
Editors: Lee Craig, Eloise Pulos
Production Manager: David Dodge
Design: Rob Weidemann
Layout and Production: Jau-Ruey Marvin
Cover Illustration: Bat Star, by Ian Sheldon
Cartography: Greg Brown
Illustrations: Ian Sheldon
Separations and Film: Elite Lithographers, Edmonton, Alberta, Canada

The publisher gratefully acknowledges the assistance of the
Department of Canadian Heritage.
PC: P3

CONTENTS

To Keeler Colton

To celebrate and welcome you
to the world.

May the beauty of nature embrace you,
Just as your loving parents
John and Carol always will.

ACKNOWLEDGMENTS

I am eternally grateful for the stimulating teaching of the staff of the Department of Zoology at Cambridge University. In particular, I was encouraged by Sally Corbet's enthusiasm in matters ecological, and Adrian and Laurie Friday inspired a deep sense and on-site appreciation of the beauty and complexity of the seashore environment.

I wish to extend my thanks to the staff at Lone Pine Publishing, to the editorial department and to the production team, both of which are a pleasure to work with. Rob Weidemann's outstanding design work on the first seashore guide (*Seashore of British Columbia/Seashore of the Pacific Northwest*) resulted in a beautiful and artistic book. I am grateful to Lone Pine Publishing for the opportunity to write and illustrate a book on this beautiful environment that I feel so passionately about. On this note, I would like to acknowledge all the hardworking and pioneering scientists who have increased and shared their knowledge about the West Coast, so that we can all share in its wonders.

Painted Urticina

REFERENCE GUIDE

MAMMALS

Sea Otter
to 5' • p. 32

Steller Sea Lion
to 10' • p. 33

California Sea Lion
to 8' • p. 34

Northern
Elephant Seal
to 16' • p. 35

Pacific Harbor Seal
to 6" • p. 36

High Cockscomb
to 8" • p. 37

Black Prickleback
to 12" • p. 38

Penpoint Gunnel
to 18" • p. 39

FISHES

Bay Blenny
to 5.75" • p. 40

Tidepool Sculpin
to 4" • p. 41

Smoothhead
Sculpin
to 5.5" • p. 42

Rosylip Sculpin
to 6" • p. 43

Calico Sculpin
to 2.75" • p. 44

Blackeye Goby
to 6" • p. 45

Northern Clingfish
to 6" • p. 46

Plainfin
Midshipman
to 15" • p. 47

California Grunion
to 7.5" • p. 48

Reef Surfperch
to 7" • p. 49

Grass Rockfish
to 22" • p. 50

Sand Sole
to 24.5" • p. 51

Round Stingray	White-cap Limpet	Fingered Limpet	File Limpet
to 22″ • p. 52	to 1.5″ • p. 53	to 1.25″ • p. 54	to 1.75″ • p. 55

Rough Limpet	Rough Keyhole Limpet	Giant Owl Limpet	Pacific Plate Limpet
to 1.25″ • p. 56	to 2.75″ • p. 57	to 4.5″ • p. 58	to 2.5″ • p. 59

Onyx Slipper Shell	Black Abalone	Frilled Dogwinkle	Emarginate Dogwinkle
to 2″ • p. 60	to 6″ • p. 61	to 4″ • p. 62	to 1″ • p. 63

Angled Unicorn	Dire Whelk	Sculptured Rocksnail	Lurid Rocksnail
to 1.5″ • p. 64	to 2″ • p. 65	to 0.75″ • p. 66	to 1.5″ • p. 67

Joseph's Coat Amphissa	Eastern Mud Whelk	Giant Western Nassa	Leafy Thorn Purpura
to 0.75″ • p. 68	to 1.25″ • p. 69	to 2″ • p. 70	to 3.5″ • p. 71

SNAILS

California Horn Shell
to 1.75″ • p. 72

Tinted Wentletrap
to 0.6″ • p. 73

Ringed Topshell
to 1.25″ • p. 74

Western Ribbed Topshell
to 1″ • p. 75

Black Tegula
to 1.75″ • p.76

Checkered Periwinkle
to 0.5″ • p. 77

Purple Dwarf Olive
to 1.25″ • p. 78

Striped Barrel Snail
to 0.75″ • p. 79

California Cone
to 1.5″ • p. 80

California Trivia
to 0.5″ • p. 81

Lewis's Moonsnail
to 5.5″ • p. 82

Pacific Pink Scallop
to 3.25″ • p. 83

BIVALVES

Clear Jewel Box
to 3.5″ • p. 84

Giant Rock Scallop
to 10″ • p. 85

Pacific Shipworm
shell 0.25″ • p. 86

Bent-nosed Macoma
to 3″ • p. 87

White Sand Macoma
to 4.5″ • p. 88

California Mactra
to 2″ • p. 89

Common Washington Clam
to 4.75″ • p. 90

Soft-shell Clam
to 5.5″ • p. 91

REFERENCE GUIDE

| Pacific Gaper
to 9″ • p. 92 | Nuttall's Cockle
to 5.5″ • p. 93 | Common Pacific
Littleneck
to 3″ • p. 94 | Japanese
Littleneck
to 3″ • p. 95 |

BIVALVES

Pacific Razor Clam
to 7″ • p. 96   Punctate Pandora
to 3″ • p. 97   False Pacific
Jingle Shell
to 4″ • p. 98   Native Pacific
Oyster
to 3.5″ • p. 99

CHITONS

California Mussel
to 8″ • p. 100   Blue Mussel
to 4″ • p. 101   Gumboot Chiton
to 13″ • p. 102   Black Katy Chiton
to 5″ • p. 103

Merten's Chiton
to 2″ • p. 104   Lined Chiton
to 2″ • p. 105   Mossy Chiton
to 3.5″ • p. 106   California Nuttall's
Chiton
to 2″ • p. 107

SEA SLUGS

Sea Lemon
to 8″ • p. 108   Yellow-edged
Cadlina
to 3″ • p. 109   Ring-spotted Doris
to 3.5″ • p. 110   Opalescent
Nudibranch
to 3″ • p. 111

REFERENCE GUIDE

Sea Clown Nudibranch
to 6" • p. 112

Elegant Aeolid
to 3.5" • p. 113

Hopkin's Rose
to 1.25" • p. 114

Navanax
to 8" • p. 115

Pugnacious Aeolid
to 2" • p. 116

Stubby Squid
to 5" • p. 117

Red Octopus
to 18" • p. 118

Leather Star
to 8" • p. 119

Troschel's Sea Star
to 22" • p. 120

Six-rayed Sea Star
to 3.5" • p. 121

Bat Star
to 8" • p. 122

Ochre Sea Star
to 14" • p. 123

Giant Sea Star
to 24" • p. 124

Sunflower Star
to 40" • p. 125

Stimpson's Sea Star
to 20" • p. 126

Esmark's Brittle Star
to 6" • p. 127

Spiny Brittle Star
to 15" • p. 128

Eccentric Sand Dollar
to 3.25" • p. 129

Red Sea Urchin
to 5" • p. 130

Purple Sea Urchin
to 3.5" • p. 131

REFERENCE GUIDE

Red Sea Cucumber
to 10″ • p. 132

California Stichopus
to 16″ • p. 133

White Sea Cucumber
to 4″ • p. 134

Purple-striped Pelagia
to 32″ • p. 135

Beroe's Comb Jelly
to 4.5″ • p. 136

By-the-wind Sailor
to 4″ • p. 137

Aggregating Anemone
to 3.5″ • p. 138

Giant Green Anemone
to 10″ • p. 139

Proliferating Anemone
to 2″ • p. 140

Frilled Anemone
to 18″ • p. 141

Painted Urticina
to 5″ • p. 142

Club-tipped Anemone
to 1.25″ • p. 143

Orange Cup Coral
to 0.4″ • p. 144

Red Crab
to 4.25″ • p. 145

Dungeness Crab
to 6.4″ • p. 146

Purple Shore Crab
to 2″ • p. 147

Striped Shore Crab
to 2″ • p. 148

Green Crab
to 2.5″ • p. 149

Black-clawed Mud Crab
to 1″ • p. 150

Flat Porcelain Crab
to 1″ • p. 151

REFERENCE GUIDE

CRABS

Shield-backed
Kelp Crab
to 4.75" • p. 152

Turtle Crab
to 2" • p. 153

Blue-handed
Hermit Crab
to 0.75" • p. 154

Acorn Barnacle
to 0.6" • p. 155

SMALL CRUSTACEANS

Giant Acorn
Barnacle
to 4" • p. 156

Volcano Barnacle
to 2" • p. 157

Common Goose
Barnacle
to 6" • p. 158

Leaf Barnacle
to 3.25" • p. 159

Smooth Skeleton
Shrimp
to 2" • p. 160

Barred Shrimp
to 1" • p. 161

Vosnesensky's
Isopod
to 1.4" • p. 162

Western Sea
Roach
to 1" • p. 163

California Beach
Flea
to 1.1" • p. 164

Tapered Flatworm
to 2.5" • p. 165

Variable
Nemertean
to 9' • p. 166

Fifteen-scaled
Worm
to 2.5" • p. 167

WORMS

Clam Worm
to 6" • p. 168

Red Tube Worm
to 4" • p. 169

Curly Terebellid
Worm
to 11" • p. 170

Giant Feather
Duster
to 11" • p. 171

Stearn's Sea
Spider
to 0.5" • p. 172

Kelp Encrusting
Bryozoan
variable • p. 173

Rosy Bryozoan
variable • p. 174

Ostrich Plume
Hydroid
to 4" • p. 175

Boring Sponge
to 12" • p. 176

Purple Sponge
to 36" • p. 177

Velvety Red
Sponge
to 36" • p. 178

Sea Pork
to 8" • p. 179

Monterey Stalked
Tunicate
to 10" • p. 180

Lightbulb Tunicate
to 20" • p. 181

Winged Kelp
to 10' • p. 182

Feather Boa
to 15' • p. 183

Oar Weed Kelp
to 5' • p. 184

Giant Perennial
Kelp
to 40' • p. 185

Bull Kelp
to 80' • p. 186

Sea Palm
to 20" • p. 187

Rockweed
to 20" • p. 188

Tar Spot
to 8" • p. 189

Sea Staghorn
to 16" • p. 190

Enteromorpha
Green Algae
to 10" • p. 191

Sea Lettuce
to 20" • p. 192

Nail Brush
to 3" • p. 193

Turkish Towel
to 18" • p. 194

Black Pine
to 12" • p. 195

Sea Sac
to 6" • p. 196

Iridescent
Seaweed
to 36" • p. 197

Coralline Algae
to 4" • p. 198

Encrusting Coral
variable • p. 199

Surf Grass
to 36" • p. 200

Eelgrass
to 36" • p. 201

Blobs of Tar/Oil
variable • p. 202

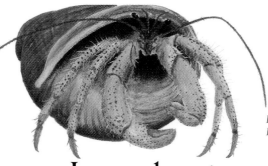

*Blue-banded
Hermit Crab*

Introduction

The temptations are always there—a beautiful coast, some rocks, some tidepools. For most of us, a walk along the beach or a holiday on the coast brings many joys. What child could resist picking up that strange stringy seaweed cast ashore by the waves, or peering into a rocky tidepool and giggling at the shy hermit crabs? For some of us, the curiosity lives with us always.

The shoreline is incredibly diverse, from extensive sandy beaches to vertical cliffs, from craggy rocks to quiet bays. In all these different landscapes, wildlife abounds. The wonderful thing about this environment is that it gives us a chance to glimpse into the ocean, a world with which we are not familiar, terrestrial animals that we are. As the tide recedes, creatures are exposed and many of them bear no resemblance to those on land. Is it a plant or animal? Maybe it is just a piece of rock. Maybe something lives in it. There are many beautiful mysteries waiting to be uncovered, waiting to be solved.

As you walk towards the shore, smell the sweetness of the sea, feel the salty spray against your skin and sway to the soothing motion of the waves washing back and forth. Remember that you are on the edge of another world. Let yourself go and discover some of the secrets of our coasts and the creatures within. The rewards are tremendous.

Sea Palm

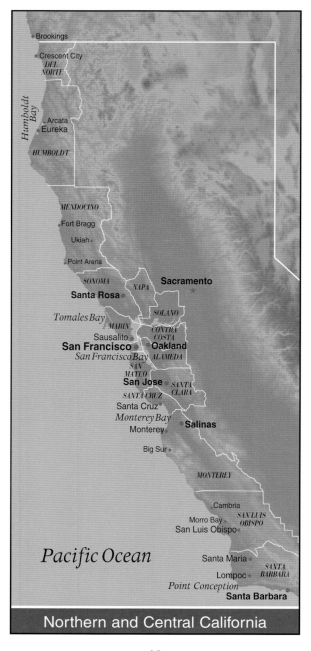

Brookings

Crescent City

DEL NORTE

Humboldt Bay

Arcata
Eureka

HUMBOLDT

MENDOCINO

Fort Bragg

Ukiah

Point Arena

SONOMA

Santa Rosa

NAPA

Sacramento

SOLANO

Tomales Bay

MARIN

Sausalito

CONTRA COSTA

San Francisco

Oakland

San Francisco Bay

ALAMEDA

SAN MATEO

San Jose

SANTA CLARA

SANTA CRUZ

Santa Cruz

Monterey Bay

Monterey

Salinas

Big Sur

MONTEREY

Cambria

Morro Bay

SAN LUIS OBISPO

San Luis Obispo

Pacific Ocean

Santa Maria

SANTA BARBARA

Lompoc

Point Conception

Santa Barbara

Northern and Central California

Orange Cup Coral

About This Book

No trip to the coast or wind-swept walk along a beach is complete without a nature guide to tell you just what it is you are looking at. Secrets abound, and while you might know that you are holding a sand dollar, do you really know what a sand dollar is and what it does with its life? This book is an easy guide to help you discover some of the stories behind the strange objects and animals found along the coasts of Northern and Central California.

Included in the guide are some of the plants and animals that you are likely to encounter as you gaze into a tidepool or wade through an eelgrass meadow. This guide is by no means exhaustive. If you had all the guides to everything you might encounter, you would probably need a truck to carry them. This book covers the basics: the plants and animals you will commonly see as you wander and wonder through the intertidal zone. You will find information about shells, sea lions, anemones, urchins, squids, seaweeds, fishes and so much more. If birds are your passion, many other guides specifically deal with these feathered friends.

Spiny Brittle Star

How to Use This Guide

At the front (p. 8) is a quick reference guide to all the groups and primary species covered by this book. The reference guide will allow you to make a visual assessment of the object of your interest. The 18 groups are identified with color bars to help you find the correct section of the book.

Each species is given a whole page with an illustration or two, text about the plant or animal and a small text box covering some of the basics, including 'Other Names,' scientific and common, given to the species. First, check that the creature resembles the one illustrated. If you are unsure, refer to the inset box and check some of the information given here. 'Range' tells you where it occurs in California, as well as in other states. 'Zone' (described shortly) refers to its position on the shore. 'Habitats' describes the types of places that the creature enjoys, perhaps the tidepools or maybe muddy sand, for example. The creature's dimensions are given so you can determine if it is the right size—maximum sizes are given; bear in mind that all things are born small and grow larger.

If the animal you are watching is green, but the illustration is red, check 'Color' in the inset box to see if it comes in different colors; many of the creatures you will encounter adapt to their environment, taking on different colors for camouflage. If you are still not satisfied, some entries have a 'Similar Species' category, referring you to other species in the book that look the same. Some similar species are also written about in the main text.

Read about the object of your fascination, and discover some of its stories as well as facts about its curious biology. Where possible, the use of strange and long scientific words has been avoided. One or two sneak their way in, and a glossary at the back (p. 203) will help you if the terms don't make sense.

Winged Kelp

The California Coast

The range covered by this guide is chiefly Northern and Central California, from the state line with Oregon to Point Conception. Many of the species will occur beyond these boundaries, and the North American range is described for each entry. Most of the creatures and seaweeds you will encounter in this region thrive in our cool waters. As you move from north to south, the water gradually gets warmer, and some of the animals will retreat into the sea to remain cool. Creatures that you commonly find intertidally in the north might never be seen intertidally in the south.

Dungeness Crab

The coastline of California is very diverse, from steep cliffs on exposed shores, to the quiet waters of the bays. Some areas are estuarine, where fresh water mixes with salty. Sandy beaches stretch into the distance and look so tempting. If you have ever tried swimming off these beautiful beaches, you know how cold the water can be. The reason for such chilly seas is that the ocean current moves southwards, bringing cold water from the far north.

Tides and the Intertidal Zone

Every coastline is shaped in some way by the tides. Two times a day the tide rises and falls. It seems remarkable that an ocean as enormous as the Pacific can move so much water around. Where does all the water go?

Both the moon and the sun are tugging at the oceans. Just as our planet has the power to attract objects, the moon and the sun do, too. The moon is closer but smaller than the sun. When the moon and sun are aligned, they both tug at the oceans, pulling the water to the side of the planet nearest them. Thus, when the tide rises in one part of the world, it is dropping somewhere else. A perfect alignment of the moon and sun

Round Stingray

creates the greatest rise and fall of the ocean. The most dramatic change in sea level along the West Coast occurs in Puget Sound, Washington, with up to 20 feet between high- and low-tide lines. Just exactly how much the tide will rise and fall depends on the exact position of the sun and moon.

This constant motion of the sea up and down a beach creates distinct zones for wildlife. Near the high-tide line, plants and animals must tolerate long periods out of water, while those at the low-tide line require long periods underwater. Some creatures and seaweeds are very particular about which part of the beach they will live in. To help you identify an animal or plant, the inset box has an entry for the 'Zone' in which it is found. Several zones are described:

Sculptured Rocksnail

Spray or Splash Zone—the uppermost part of the beach influenced by wave action. Here, the rocks only ever receive splashes from the surf or spray, and are never covered by the sea.

Upper Intertidal Zone—the uppermost band covered by the highest point of an incoming tide. Here, organisms must tolerate prolonged periods exposed to the elements.

Middle Intertidal Zone—the middle band covered half the time by the tides. More organisms are able to survive here, because they are not exposed to drying conditions for too long.

Lower Intertidal Zone—the lowest part of the beach that is only uncovered for a short period of time. Here, growth is luxuriant, because many organisms can tolerate the short exposure to air.

Also included under 'Zone' are 'inshore' and 'open water,' where inshore means the creature will come close to the shoreline, and open water means they are usually out in the seas far from the shore.

The high-tide line is the highest point that the sea will reach on the incoming tide; the low-tide line is the point at which the sea is as far out as it will go. Once the tide reaches its lowest point, it begins to come in, or rise, again. Below the low-tide line is the **Subtidal Zone**, which is never exposed by a receding tide. The sealife in this zone can be very different because it is never exposed to the rigors of the air, sun, frosts and rain or the presence of beachcombers.

Merten's Chiton

Beachcombing
What to Do and What Not to Do

So much fun is to be had from beachcombing, but there are a number of important points to remember to ensure that it is a success and pleasure for you and for those who come after you.

Choosing the right location is a good start. While all coastlines will have their wildlife, some will be better than others. Gently sloping, rocky beaches riddled with tide-pools are perhaps the most rewarding. But don't count out wading through an eelgrass meadow, or hiking the fringes of a quiet bay either. Safety is a concern—you don't want to fall off a cliff, be swept away by a large wave or get stuck in estuarine mud when the tide starts to come in.

Be very wary of the tides, and learn how to read the tide tables that are posted in national parks and at information offices in ports and towns. Tide tables will help you decide what time of day to go to the beach—aim for an ebb tide, because it is safer to follow the water receding out to the low-tide line, than to be chased back up the beach by an advancing tide. Where the shore is very flat the tide can race in, cutting you off on a rocky ledge or sand bar. Be vigilant!

Some organisms, such as the California Mussel (p. 100), thrive where the surf is strongest and waves pound the shores, and these are useful indicators of 'crazy surf.' Freak waves do happen, and they take their victims from time to time. Don't be one of them. It is very easy to become so engrossed in a tidepool that you lose all sense of time and place, and before you know it, the tide is rushing in with full force. With this caution in mind, beachcombing is best done in a group in case of accidents, and also because your treasured finds can be more enjoyable when shared with others.

The treasures of beach-combing come small and large. Bring a pail and a hand lens to study the small creatures. Some of these creatures will only emerge from their homes when underwater. A hand lens will help you see the tiny animals that make up a

Volcano Barnacle

bryozoan colony, for example. And bring this book! It will help you identify and learn about the shore.

Many people believe that they can take some of their finds home. First, think about where you are— removal is forbidden in many locations. Know the local laws and regulations. Second, think about the luckless victim of your interest. Many sea stars have been transported home in the hope that they will dry and make eye-catching souvenirs. They don't. They rot, they smell bad, and you kill them. Similarly, don't transfer organisms to fresh water—that will kill them, too. In short, resist the temptation to take anything. The rocky tidepool is home for shorelife, and they would probably rather stay there.

Leather Star

Many plants and animals of the ocean are considered fine eating. If you are tempted to try them out, never harvest every one in sight. Too many creatures have succumbed to exploitation. It is important to check local regulations regarding sizes of shellfish that are harvested— most have a minimum size requirement to meet before they can be collected. Also, check for information about 'red tide,' which poisons some shellfish, and if you eat them you might well regret it. If you want to harvest some sea-weed, don't pull up the whole plant, just trim off part of the plant so that it can still grow and reproduce.

Most important of all, respect the shoreline. It is not yours. You do not own the wildlife on it. Living creatures deserve your love and attention; try not to interfere. Do turn over rocks to see what is hiding underneath, and do put these rocks back the way you found them, in their original position so the animals feel protected once more. Watch out for creatures as you clamber about the rocks. It is tempting to use mussel and barnacle beds for good foot-ing on steep rocks. Each step you take will kill. A small chip off a mussel shell opens it up to the elements and to predation.

Beaches make popular locations for picnics. Make sure you take all your garbage home with you. Plastic waste is hazardous to wildlife and broken glass might end up

Bay Blenny

in the foot of the next beachcomber to follow you. Don't just take your own garbage home with you, but remove what other people have left behind. Sadly, our oceans have long been seen as giant refuse pits, with tons of garbage cast from ships. This garbage floats ashore in its various forms, sometimes dangerous, always ugly.

Nuttall's Cockle

Shorelife to Discover

The shorelife of the intertidal zone comes in so many shapes and sizes that an overview of each group might help you understand where it fits in with the natural order of things. Some animals look so strange you would be forgiven for thinking that they are plants!

There are animals with backbones (vertebrates), there are animals without backbones (invertebrates) and there are seaweeds (plants). The few vertebrates you will discover are the fishes and mammals, but by far the majority of the creatures you will encounter are invertebrates. The invertebrates covered in this guide fall into distinct groups: mollusks, echinoderms, cnidarians, crustaceans, worms and other small organisms.

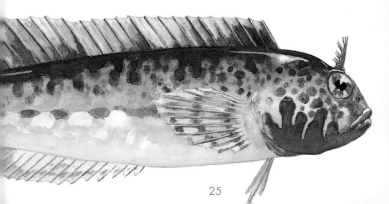

Mollusks

The largest group covered by this guide is the mollusks, and it includes some very different organisms indeed. It is hard to believe, for example, that the massive octopus is related to a limpet stuck on a rock. A mollusk is typified by a soft body and a hard shell for protection (though some mollusks have lost this shell). Lining the internal side of the shell is soft tissue called the 'mantle,' and this mantle creates a cavity in which gills for breathing are located. There are distinct groups of mollusks: limpets and snails (the gastropods); bivalves; chitons (the polyplacophorans); sea slugs (the nudibranchs); and squids and octopus (the cephalopods).

Gastropods have one large sucking foot and a shell of various forms. The Polyplacophorans are limpet-like with their huge sucking foot, but they have a line of eight separate articulating plates down the back. The bivalves are all the clams, oysters and scallops. They are grouped together because they all have two valves, or shells, which enclose the soft body of the animal, and a muscular foot often used for burrowing. The nudibranchs are also gastropods, but they have lost their shell and rely on other means to protect themselves. The least likely looking mollusks are the squids and octopus, called cephalopods. Highly intelligent and active, they are the most advanced of all the mollusks.

The dietary preferences of mollusks are as varied as their forms. Some mollusks graze on microscopic algae; some snails ferociously prey on other snails; squids grapple with lively prey; and bivalves, which are filter feeders, suck water into the mantle cavity to sift it for tiny particles.

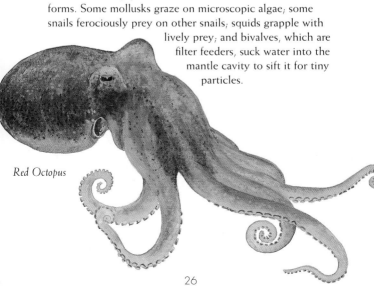

Red Octopus

Giant Sea Star

Echinoderms

'Echinoderm' means spiny skin, and this group of animals is strictly marine. It includes the sea stars, brittle stars, sea urchins and sea cucumbers. These creatures are ancient animals of prehistoric times, and are still very successful today. They have radial symmetry, usually based on the form of a five-pointed star.

Seawater is pumped around the body to hydraulically power the tiny tube feet that move the animals around. Their firm structure is given by a calcareous skeleton most obvious in dead sea urchins, such as the Eccentric Sand Dollar (p. 129). Echinoderms have the remarkable ability to regenerate limbs. A spine can regrow on an urchin, and a whole leg can grow back on a sea star—however, this ability does not give you license to go pulling them to pieces!

Cnidarians

Cnidarians are the soft, jelly-like animals of the sea. They include the jellyfish, sea anemones and corals. They are typified by having stinging tentacles to capture their prey. The sting comes from the tiny cells, called 'nematocysts,' lining the tentacles. Corals are soft-bodied animals that lay down a calcareous base to which they attach. It is the coral 'skeletons' that make up the elaborate reefs in tropical waters. Hydroids resemble extremely small colonies of corals and occur in many different forms. This guide has only one species of coral.

Aggregating Anemone

Crustaceans

These animals have jointed limbs
and hard outer skins, or shells. They
are a very successful group, and are
best represented by the crabs.
Shrimps, barnacles and beach
fleas are also crustaceans, however, and their enormously diverse
forms are reflected in the many
different lifestyles and eating habits.
Having a tough outer skeleton has a
distinct disadvantage—how do you grow? Crabs, for example, have overcome this growth problem by molting period-
ically. They lose the old, hard skin for a new, more flexible
one that gradually hardens. Molting is a dangerous time for
crustaceans, because their usually tough outer skin momen-
tarily becomes soft and vulnerable. The cast-off skeletons of
crabs frequently wash ashore in great numbers.

Barred Shrimp

Worms

Most of the worms in this guide are annelid worms.
These segmented creatures have many appendages that
assist in walking and breathing. Some wander and are fero-
cious predators, while others, such as Red Tube Worms
(p. 169), stay put, build a tube around themselves and filter
the water with a pretty fan of feather-like appendages on
the head. Other worms featured include the Variable
Nemertean (p. 166), which is a very different
kind of worm, not related to the annelids.
Nemerteans do not have distinct seg-
ments, but have one long, stretchy
body. The Tapered Flatworm (p. 165)
belongs to another group of worms
called the platy-
helminths. These
flatworms can spread
themselves so thinly
that they all but
disappear.

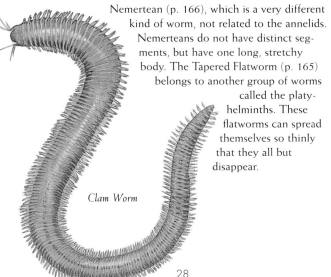

Clam Worm

Other Small Organisms

There are many other less distinct groups to be found along the seashore. These groups include the pycnogonids, bryozoans, poriferans and urochordates.

Pycnogonids are commonly called sea spiders. These creepy creatures are not related to the true spiders (arachnids) that we know so well on land. Only one species of pycnogonid is represented in this guide.

Bryozoans, sometimes called moss animals, are so small that they can be missed or mistaken for something else. Bryozoans are tiny colonial animals that build walled homes of calcium carbonate about them. As the colony expands, it takes on a distinctive form particular to the type of bryozoan. There are many different kinds, and colonies can be shaped like trees, bushes and flat encrustations or grow convincingly as corals. They are filter feeders, using tentacles that extend from their little homes.

Poriferans are simple sponges. They are animals represented by loose aggregations of cells organized to filter water and extract the tiny particles of food from it. Usually, the surface of a sponge is covered in tiny pores through which water passes in and out. Typically, a sponge grows flat in the intertidal zone, but in deeper calmer water it can be much more elaborate and grows to great sizes. Many sponges have tiny silica strands to serve as a skeleton, or support. These small crystals are often used by nudibranchs when they have been ingested.

Urochordates are peculiar animals that actually bear some resemblance and connection to humans—for at least part of their lives. They are classified in the same large group as us, the chordates, but have gone off in their own direction in evolutionary terms. When they are very young and free swimming, they have gills, a little tail and a nerve cord running down their back. They somewhat resemble tadpoles or humans first developing as embryos. Soon all

Monterey Stalked Tunicate

that changes, and what looks like it is going to be an advanced and extraordinary animal, loses all these features, settles down on a rock and becomes a strange blob of flesh that filters water throughout its life. They can be solitary or live in colonies, and are called sea squirts or tunicates.

Seaweeds

The plants of the intertidal zone come in various shapes and sizes, and have been classified accordingly. There are four groups to consider. Algae are divided into three principal groups: brown, green and red. The fourth group, the flowering plants, is only represented by a few grass-like plants in the sea. Collectively, these algae and flowering plants are commonly known as seaweeds.

Algae

The large family of brown algae includes the magnificent kelps. The color is determined by the dominant pigments for photosynthesis, and they usually come in shades of brown, although some retain rich olive-green colors. The kelps are very successful, forming huge forests just offshore.

The green algae family includes the fleshy, green algae of the intertidal zone. The dominant pigments are

Giant Perennial Kelp

Bull Kelp

used to harness the energy from the sun (photosynthesis) and make the algae green. Some are very bright green, while others can be so dark they appear to be black.

Just to confuse the issue of classification, the red algae family can come in shades of red, brown, green or blue. In addition, some have incorporated calcium carbonate into their structures, taking on hard and crusty coralline forms. Some of the red algae can be very beautifully and richly colored, and the exact color they have depends on the balance of the pigments used in photosynthesis.

Flowering Plants

Do not expect to find a sunflower or geranium, but look out for grass-like plants growing in quiet bays or on rocky shores. These are Eelgrass (p. 201) and Surf Grass (p. 200). They are flowering plants like those on land, with a root system and neat rows of inconspicuous flowers tucked in close to the stem. For pollination, they rely on the sea to carry pollen from one flower to the next, just in the same way as terrestrial grasses rely on the wind.

Eelgrass

Sea Otter

ENHYDRA LUTRIS

Little surpasses the beauty of a playful and intelligent Sea Otter baby nestled on the furry belly of its floating mother. The Sea Otter was once persecuted to the point of extinction, and its thick pelt, vital for chilly waters, made it a popular animal for trapping. Now protected and making a strong recovery, the Sea Otter is a cherished sight for wildlife watchers —Monterey Bay is one of the best places to observe it —and its presence is evidence of a healthy ecosystem. Watch out for the River Otter (*Lutra canadensis*), with its longer tail and slimmer build, which also takes to the seas.

RANGE: California, Washington, British Columbia, Alaska; scattered

ZONE: inshore; occasionally on shore

HABITATS: kelp beds

LENGTH: 5 ft

WEIGHT: 100 lb

Five feet long and needing copious quantities of fuel to keep warm, the Sea Otter has a voracious appetite for shellfish, crabs, urchins and fishes. When the Sea Otter had all but been annihilated, sea urchins grew in such numbers that the kelp forests could not regenerate. With the otter now returning, the kelp forests are healthy and balanced once again. Fisheries still fear the otter's huge appetite, and although protected by law, the Sea Otter is a sad victim of oil spills—the fur's waterproof and insulating qualities are destroyed when oil seeps into it.

Steller Sea Lion
EUMETOPIAS JUBATUS

Steller Sea Lions are a treat to see in summer when they frequently haul themselves out onto rocks, but they move north, out of state, after breeding. The massive bulls grow to some 10 feet in length and can weigh over 2200 pounds. Such massiveness wins cows, so watch for the dominant male amidst his harem—the dainty females are a mere third of the bull's bulk. The male is also noticeable for his thick neck and golden-brown hues, whereas the females are darker. This sea lion is larger and lighter in color than the California Sea Lion (the male of which has a prominent ridge on his forehead), and does not bark as much.

Rather sensitive to people approaching, Steller Sea Lions will readily dive into the water, where they feel safer, and observe you from a distance. Poor weather also drives them in, and long feeding trips to dine on fish might even take them up rivers. For reasons unknown, the population of this magnificent animal is diminishing. It is thought that competition with humans for certain fish might be one cause—sea lions just cannot compete with our huge nets.

OTHER NAME: Northern Sea Lion

RANGE: Southern California to Alaska; scattered

ZONE: intertidal to open water

HABITATS: rocky shores of open coasts

LENGTH: male to 10 ft; female to 7 ft

WEIGHT: male to 2200 lb; female to 800 lb

SIMILAR SPECIES: California Sea Lion (p. 34)

California Sea Lion

ZALOPHUS CALIFORNIANUS

Fun-loving performers, California Sea Lions are bold and sometimes daring. They are commonly used in marine aquariums to perform tricks, but in the wild they are just as capable of amusing themselves, taking delight in flinging kelp around and bodysurfing in large waves. Their loud bark can often be heard from afar. Monterey is a good place to get a close look at these sea lions. Females stay at the breeding grounds on offshore islands in Southern California year-round, while the males move north, as far as Canada, after breeding. At haul-outs on sandy beaches and reefs, they will often mix with other seals and sea lions.

This sea lion resembles the Steller Sea Lion, but the California Sea Lion is darker and smaller, and the male has a prominent ridge on his forehead, a feature lacking in the Steller Sea Lion. The flippers are hairless and black, helping this mammal to swim swiftly and dive to the impressive depths of 800 feet in its quest for fish and squid. Flat reefs and rocky shores make for great sea lion beach parties, often quite raucous! The Steller Sea Lions are more reserved about barking.

RANGE: Southern California to British Columbia

ZONE: intertidal to open water

HABITATS: rocky shores; beaches

LENGTH: male to 8 ft; female to 6.5 ft

WEIGHT: male to 750 lb; female to 250 lb

SIMILAR SPECIES: Steller Sea Lion (p. 33)

Northern Elephant Seal

MIROUNGA ANGUSTIROSTRIS

Aside from beached whales, the Northern Elephant Seal is the largest mammal a beachcomber is likely to encounter. Massively intimidating, this hefty beast gets its name from the male's extended snout. Early in the year the huge males and comparatively tiny females come ashore to breed. During the breeding season the male's snout is inflated, appearing larger than usual. Males try to impress one another, and frequently scar each other's chest and thickened neck in the process. One of the best sites to witness these spectacular animals is in Año Nuevo State Park in San Mateo County.

In summer months the males migrate northwards from their breeding grounds in search of rich feeding and a place to molt. During the molting season, they are seen lounging around on rocky shores and islands, seldom doing much at all. Occasional sightings are made in quiet inland waters, but open seas are preferred, and here they can dive to staggering depths of 5000 feet for an hour or more. They feed on fishes, squids, octopus and even the occasional shark! Once almost wiped out by over-hunting for their oily skin, Northern Elephant Seals have since made a dramatic recovery.

RANGE: Southern California to Alaska

ZONE: intertidal to open water

HABITATS: rocky shores; isolated beaches

LENGTH: male to 16 ft; female to 9 ft

WEIGHT: male to 5000 !b; female to 2000 lb

Pacific Harbor Seal
PHOCA VITULINA

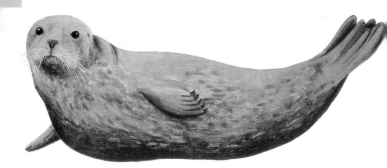

These handsome harbor seals are mammals that are commonly seen close to human activity. Found from the open coast into protected bays as well as estuaries and up rivers, they have the confidence to enter harbors and swim beside boats, while curiously observing the contents. Pacific Harbor Seals come in a variety of colors from white to black, the most common combination being a buff color flecked with darker spots.

OTHER NAME: Leopard Seal

RANGE: California to Alaska

ZONE: intertidal to open water

HABITATS: rocky shores; beaches; estuaries; harbors

LENGTH: male to 6 ft; female to 5.5 ft

WEIGHT: male to 300 lb; female to 175 lb

When the tide is in, they are actively diving and hunting, eating all manner of fishes. They are partial to the occasional clam or squid. At low tide they haul out onto rocky platforms to sunbathe, where they can be seen singly or in groups. Pacific Harbor Seals always have one eye open for humans that come too close. When afraid, the seals readily dive into water. Underwater, however, they are in their element, and can be quite curious and friendly with divers. They make themselves unpopular with fishermen, unfortunately, because they cunningly steal fishes from nets. They are, in turn, the prey of Orcas (killer whales) and even suffer the hungry attentions of the Northern Elephant Seal (p. 35).

High Cockscomb
ANOPLARCHUS PURPURESCENS

Slippery as an eel and as hard to handle, this fish is a common sight under rocks in tidepools and among stones on cobble beaches. When turning rocks, you might even find a little gathering of this variably colored fish, which can be olive, brown or a stunning rich purple-black that offsets the red fins.

The High Cockscomb frequently sports two attractive red designer stripes by the eye and a strange crest on its head. Males have brightly colored fins to impress the females, who are not so brightly colored. Laying as many as 3000 eggs among the rocks, the female will wrap herself around the eggs and guard them lovingly until they hatch. Meanwhile, the philandering male abandons her, perhaps for another mate. Both male and female fall prey to garter snakes that wander down to the shore at low tide in search of these tasty morsels.

OTHER NAMES: Cockscomb Prickleback; Crested Blenny

RANGE: Southern California to Alaska

ZONE: lower intertidal; subtidal to 20 ft

HABITATS: under rocks; tide-pools; sheltered coasts; cobble beaches

LENGTH: to 8 in

COLOR: variable

SIMILAR SPECIES: Black Prickleback (p. 38)

The High Cockscomb is frequently confused with the Slender Cockscomb (*A. insignis*), which, as its name implies, is somewhat thinner and has a smaller crest. Young Monkey-face Pricklebacks (*Cebidichthys violaceus*) lack the spiny texture in the dorsal fin and grow much larger.

Black Prickleback

XIPHISTER ATROPURPUREUS

Chocolate-brown or black, this lithe, eel-like fish has some distinctive markings on the face that help us to identify it. Two comical, black bands descend from the eye and are bordered in white. The similar Rock Prickleback (*X. mucosus*) has eye bands that are pale and bordered in black. At the base of the tail, most Black Pricklebacks have a white band. The pectoral fin just behind the gills is so small as to be hardly noticeable.

OTHER NAME: Black Blenny

RANGE: Southern California to Alaska

ZONE: lower intertidal; subtidal to 25 ft

HABITATS: tidepools; under rocks; rocky shores

LENGTH: to 12 in

COLOR: dark red-brown to black

SIMILAR SPECIES: High Cockscomb (p. 37)

Black Pricklebacks are common fish when the tide is out. Larger ones will tend to hide under rocks, while the younger, smaller pricklebacks can be seen in tidepools. Be careful when turning rocks because several males might be underneath, all wrapped around their egg masses. They patiently wait up to three weeks for the eggs to hatch. Be especially careful when placing the rock back where it was. Some land animals, such as garter snakes and feisty minks, will come down at low tide to dine on sheltering pricklebacks.

Penpoint Gunnel
A P O D I C H T H Y S   F L A V I D U S

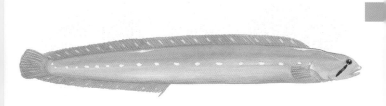

Wriggling and writhing like an eel, the Penpoint Gunnel is hard to handle. This strikingly colored fish hides among seaweeds of the intertidal zone. Green, yellow, red or even brown, this fish will take on the colors of its environment—so expect to find a red Penpoint Gunnel in red seaweed. Also hunt for it in tidepools and under rocks. Its name alludes to the long spine at the front of the anal fin along the fish's underside. Other features include the black eye-line and a dark or light line of dots along its flank.

This fish is seldom seen, despite being common in Northern California. The Penpoint Gunnel is less abundant to the south. A small mouth means it seldom takes a bite on hooked bait, and a slender build saves the gunnel from being eaten by fish-hungry anglers. Crustaceans and mollusks make up its diet. In winter they retreat under rocks, where they can sometimes be found wrapped tenderly around a white egg mass. The smaller Rockweed Gunnel (*Xererpes fucorum*) lacks the black eye-line, but shares the same habitats.

RANGE: Southern California to Alaska

ZONE: middle to lower intertidal

HABITATS: under rocks; eelgrass beds; tidepools

LENGTH: to 18 in

COLOR: green, yellow, red or brown

Bay Blenny

HYPSOBLENNIUS GENTILIS

Most blennies enjoy warmer waters, but the Bay Blenny is one of the few that ventures into the cool waters of Central California, if only as far north as Monterey Bay. This fish is aggressive and energetic, and is even known to defend its burrow from overly curious divers. It is common in the intertidal zone, darting about in tidepools where it grazes on algae and sessile invertebrates stuck on the rocks.

RANGE: Central and Southern California

ZONE: intertidal; subtidal to 80 ft

HABITATS: bays; estuaries

LENGTH: to 5.75 in

COLOR: brown and green; mottled

The male is most glamorously marked in the breeding season, and boasts a vibrant splash of red underneath the chin, as well as splashes of color on the first part of the dorsal fin that stretches all the way down the back of the fish. The female has a blue spot where the male has red. The male entices a female into his burrow by wagging his colorful chin about. If the female succumbs to his advances, she lays eggs that the male then guards until they hatch. Non-breeding males and females are generally a mottled green or brown on the back and much paler underneath. Look for the prominent cirri above the eye, much like an elaborate eyebrow.

Tidepool Sculpin
OLIGOCOTTUS MACULOSUS

When you stare into tidepools, you are sure to notice this hardy sculpin, which can put up with the rigors of tidepool life: steaming hot one day, bitterly cold the next. A lively character confined in a small world, the Tidepool Sculpin depends on camouflage for protection. The excellent coloration makes it hard to see until it darts about. These sculpins are definitely fishes with attitude, and taking the time to watch them is a joy. Perhaps most extraordinary is their ability to return to their home pool— even when taken as much as 330 feet away.

Colors are variable, gray-greens being more common. Keep in mind that if the tide-pool is predominantly one color,

RANGE: Southern California to Alaska
ZONE: middle to upper intertidal
HABITATS: tidepools
LENGTH: to 4 in
COLOR: variable
SIMILAR SPECIES: Smoothhead Sculpin (p. 42)

then this scaleless sculpin will match that color. To help blend even further with its habitat, the sculpin's large fins are almost transparent, with occasional markings. When resting, the dorsal fins fall back flush with the body. Down the back there are sometimes several 'saddles' darker in color. This sculpin is easily confused with the Fluffy Sculpin (O. snyderi), which has more hair-like growths on both its face and body.

Smoothhead Sculpin

ARTEDIUS LATERALIS

The Smoothhead Sculpin is much larger than the Tide-pool Sculpin. Other features that might help you identify this fish from the many other confusing species of sculpins include a long, pointed face, large mouth and small eyes set well back. This sculpin is more common in the north of its range, where it can be found in tidepools and under rocks. Masterful green and brown coloration can make it very hard to distinguish from its environment. Most of the fins have dark barring and on the upper surfaces the body has scales—these features are lacking in the Tidepool Sculpin.

RANGE: Southern California to Alaska

ZONE: middle to lower intertidal; subtidal to 43 ft

HABITATS: tidepools; rocky shores

LENGTH: to 5.5 in

COLOR: green to brown

SIMILAR SPECIES: Tidepool Sculpin (p. 41)

The Smoothhead Sculpin's diet consists of small crusta-ceans, including shrimps and crabs. Young fishes are also con-sumed, and, much to the annoyance of anglers, the sculpins are cunning enough to remove the bait from hooks without being caught themselves. Other signs to look out for include the masses of red eggs tucked away near rocks for protection in tidepools—the eggs are laid during winter months.

Rosylip Sculpin
ASCELICHTHYS RHODORUS

Splashes of red adorn the lips and fringe the upper edge of the dorsal fin of the Rosylip Sculpin. Richly colored in olive-browns and cinnamon, it can be a little hard to notice, because this sculpin is not so keen to move, preferring to rely on camouflage and stillness for protection. The body is long compared to other sculpins, and lacks scales, making it very smooth. The dark brown fins have lighter edges. One of the best distinguishing features is the lack of a pelvic fin, which in other sculpins drops down from the underside. A small cirrus, or hair-like projection, rises on top of the head near the eye.

RANGE: Central California to Alaska

ZONE: upper to lower intertidal; subtidal to 33 ft

HABITATS: tidepools; under rocks; gravel; eelgrass beds

LENGTH: to 6 in

COLOR: brown

The best places to encounter this pretty face are in tidepools, where they are abundant, and under rocks at low tide. Gravel beaches and dense eelgrass beds are also favored. This sculpin can be very common in some parts of its range. The Rosylip Sculpin seldom seizes baited hooks, and if it did, it would surely just anger anglers, because its small size makes it worthless for eating.

Calico Sculpin

CLINOCOTTUS EMBRYUM

This sculpin gets its name from its beautiful and colorful markings. Although frequently occurring in various shades of red, the Calico Sculpin is sometimes green; all variations are typified by six dark saddles down the back. On the lower flanks the color fades and worm-like markings, or vermiculations, replace the rich colors. Other distinctive markings include dark bars radiating from the eye, bars across the fins and black-tipped lips.

OTHER NAME: Mossy Sculpin

RANGE: Central California to Alaska

ZONE: middle intertidal to subtidal

HABITATS: tidepools; rocky shores

LENGTH: to 2.75 in

COLOR: green, pink, red, maroon

SIMILAR SPECIES: Tidepool Sculpin (p. 41), Smoothhead Sculpin (p. 42)

This sculpin also goes by the descriptive name of Mossy Sculpin, a name that relates to the bundles and lines of cirri, hair-like growths, on and down the sides of the head. One of the better places to hunt down this elusive sculpin is among the encrusting growths of Coralline Algae in tidepools along rocky ocean coasts.

While hunting you are sure to come across a host of sculpins, many of which adopt the color of their tidepool for protection. All of these things make for really tough times when it comes to identifying exactly which sculpins are resident. Be sure to compare your find with other sculpins in this guide.

Blackeye Goby
CORYPHOPTERUS NICHOLSI

Pretty in pinks, tans and other pale colors, this small fish sports a number of distinguishing features. A large, dark eye and black border to the first dorsal fin stand out against the pale body covered in large scales. Just underneath the eye is a faint iridescent blue patch, and along the top of the head is a fleshy ridge. Breeding males have dark pelvic fins, the very sight of which can sometimes be enough to lure a female into a cave. Usually it takes a bit of a dance to convince a female to enter a male's abode, where she then lays her eggs. After fertilization, the male guards the eggs until they hatch.

OTHER NAMES: Crested Goby; Bluespot Goby

RANGE: Southern California to Alaska

ZONE: lower intertidal; subtidal to 450 ft

HABITATS: tidepools; rocks and sand

LENGTH: to 6 in

COLOR: tan, brown, yellow, pink; sometimes speckled

The best goby sites are where rocks and sand meet, because the male can excavate a burrow to his liking beneath the rock. He will courageously defend this site by puffing up his cheeks and looking large. If that fails, he can always retreat into the burrow for protection. Curiously, these feisty males started life as females, changing sex as they aged. Another goby that will also be seen darting into burrows (in this case left by other animals) is the pale gray Arrow Goby (*Clevelandia ios*).

Northern Clingfish
G O B I E S O X   M A E A N D R I C U S

An oversized tadpole best describes this intertidal fish. The broad, flattened head and narrow, tapered body are very distinctive. Specially modified fins on the underside of the head allow the tenacious Northern Clingfish to suck onto the underside of rocks in shallow water. Lift a rock gently and look at the underside to see if any clingfishes are hanging on for their lives. The sucking disc on the underside is so successful that it can be a challenge to remove the fish. If you succeed, place it on the palm of your hand and hold it upside down—these fishes really do cling!

OTHER NAME: Flathead Clingfish

RANGE: Southern California to Alaska

ZONE: intertidal; subtidal to 26 ft

HABITATS: under rocks and kelp

LENGTH: to 6 in

COLOR: variable red and brown; mottled

The clingfish can also be found under kelp. It forages on other under-rock inhabitants, especially small crustaceans, mollusks and worms. The female lays a clutch of eggs on the underside of a rock, and the male will guard the eggs until they hatch. The color of a clingfish is variable, from light and dark browns and reds, with mottling and a pale bridge usually connecting the eyes. These fishes are common but frequently overlooked because of their dark colors and habit of hiding under rocks.

Plainfin Midshipman

PORICHTHYS NOTATUS

Summer residents of Sausalito (San Francisco Bay) know the antics of the Plainfin Midshipman all too well. In late spring, the males take up temporary residence in the shallows near houseboats. Here, they hum the night away, causing distress to tired humans. This strange buzz, croak or, at a real stretch of the imagination, song is made by the fish squeezing air around its swim bladder (a gas-filled organ that allows the fish to adjust its buoyancy). Females find this sound more attractive than humans do, and come to lay their eggs. Be sure to check near rocks at low tide for males protecting their egg masses.

OTHER NAME: Northern Midshipman; Singing Toadfish
RANGE: California to Alaska
ZONE: lower intertidal; subtidal to 1200 ft
HABITATS: bays; estuaries; under rocks
LENGTH: to 15 in
COLOR: green, brown or purplish

This depressed-looking fish has many tiny, light organs, or photophores, on its underside. These photophores will flash when the fish is handled, but their function might be for courtship or to light up the underside to make the fish look pale against the brighter light above. The Plainfin Midshipman is active by night, preferring to remain buried by day, with its bulbous eyes poking through the muddy sand. Perhaps it looks sad because it seems just about everything eats it. Sea lions, birds, other fishes and many others dine on it, but remarkably, it is not so popular among fish-eating humans.

California Grunion
LEURESTHES TENUIS

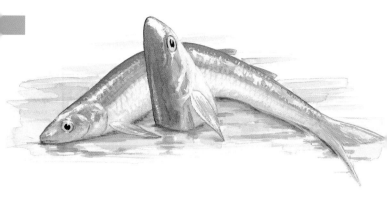

From March through August, when the moon is full and spring tide is at its highest, a strange phenomenon can be witnessed by night. On sandy beaches south of Monterey Bay, the California Grunion comes ashore and crowds of people gather to watch. Driven by an urge to crawl out onto the beach to lay their eggs, these slippery, silvery fishes are brought in by the waves and remain on the sand where they dance and flip about. The females bury themselves tail first into the moist sand, while the males wrap themselves against the females. This action allows the male's sperm to drain down the body of the female and fertilize the eggs deep in the sand where they are protected. At the next high tide, the eggs hatch. Once the eggs have been laid and fertilized, these fishes leave with the next big wave.

SPAWNING RANGE: Monterey Bay to Southern California

ZONE: low-tide line; subtidal to 60 ft

HABITATS: sandy beaches; open ocean

LENGTH: to 7.5 in

COLOR: silvery-blue and green

With a strong desire to dine on these fishy creatures, people gather in great numbers to catch them, but also just to watch. Fortunately for this seething mass of fishes, the law dictates that anglers are only allowed to catch California Grunions with their bare hands. This restriction gives these fishes some chance at returning to the open water just offshore.

Reef Surfperch

MICROMETRUS AURORA

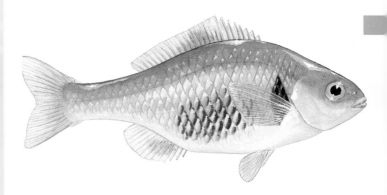

This cheerful little fish can be commonly seen in the larger tidepools of California and in the shallow subtidal waters of rocky shores as far north as Tomales Bay. Schools of Reef Surfperch gather in the rocky shallows near seaweeds, where they feed on algae and small invertebrates. Many fishes are in the same family as the Reef Surfperch, but this surfperch is one of the few that gets caught in large tidepools and swims near enough to the shore to be accessible to the curious beachcomber.

OTHER NAME: Reefperch

RANGE: south of Tomales Bay

ZONE: lower intertidal; subtidal to 30 ft

HABITATS: tidepools; rocky shores

LENGTH: to 7 in

COLOR: blue-green, silver; with black and gold markings

The coloring of this fish is typical of many fishes that don't want to be seen too easily. The back of the fish is blue-green so that it is hard for predators to detect the fish from above. Meanwhile, predators beneath the Reef Surfperch have a hard time seeing it because its belly is pale, to match the bright light from the surface. Distinctive markings on the Reef Surfperch include a bold splash of black behind each gill and pectoral fin, as well as a patch of black-edged scales along the lower sides. The large scales are further enhanced by a band of gold stretching almost from head to tail.

Grass Rockfish
SEBASTES RASTRELLIGER

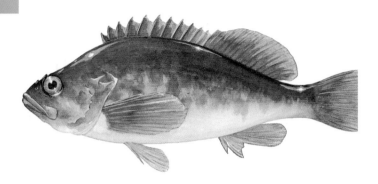

Just offshore along rocky coastlines begins the world of the rockfishes. There are many different species of these chunky, spiny fish, but the one the beachcomber is likely to encounter is the Grass Rockfish. Dark green and mottled, the fish is colored this way to help it blend in with kelp and eelgrass beds where it likes to hang out. In some fishes, the lower fins might be tinged with pink.

OTHER NAME: Grass Rockcod

RANGE: California to Oregon

ZONE: lower intertidal; subtidal to 150 ft

HABITATS: tidepools; rocky shores

LENGTH: to 22 in

COLOR: mottled dark green

At low tide it is possible to see the Grass Rockfish in large tidepools. Another sure bet for a close encounter with one is to become friendly with an angler; this is a popular fish to haul out and eat. Its tendency to hang out close to the shore makes it accessible to anglers, and its big size makes it worth the fisher's effort. If a lucky rockfish escapes these baited hooks, it can live to a reported 17 years, during which time it has plenty of opportunity to dine on crabs, octopuses and other fishes. The sad-looking Plainfin Mid-shipman (p. 47) falls prey to the Grass Rockfish when it enters rockfish territory to spawn.

50

Sand Sole

PSETTICHTHYS MELANOSTICTUS

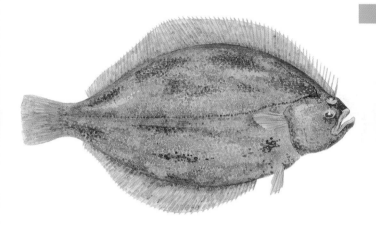

This flatfish is sometimes stranded in sandy tidepools. The Sand Sole matches the color of the sand so well—and flaps its fins and partially buries itself—that you would be forgiven for thinking that there is nothing in the empty-looking tidepool. An older, larger Sand Sole will seldom be found in these pools, because it moves into deeper water.

The Sand Sole is different from other flatfish or flounders in that the first several sharp rays on the dorsal fin have no membrane between them. This fish is right-eyed, meaning that the upper surface is always the right-hand side of the fish. Try to think of flatfish as tall, thin fishes that decided to flop over on one side, and so had to move an eye over to the other side of their faces. The upper surface is colored and the underside is pale. The Sand Sole is frequently caught by inshore anglers and makes for fine dining, which gives it some market value. Fortunately for the Sand Sole, its preference for shallow waters protects it from large-scale commercial fisheries.

RANGE: Southern California to Alaska

ZONE: inshore; subtidal to 600 ft

HABITATS: sandy tidepools; sandy bottoms

LENGTH: to 24.5 in

COLOR: black-speckled tan, brown

Round Stingray
UROLOPHUS HALLERI

It is the luckless recreational bather that steps on the Round Stingray—this stinging fish does not actively pursue bathers, but it will sting if stepped on. The sting is located on the short tail, and can inflict quite a lot of pain. Shuffle your feet along as you move, and the stingray will glide out of your way.

This fish is the most common of stingrays in California waters, and is more abundant from Monterey Bay southwards. Unfortunately for beachgoers, stingrays decide to move inshore during summer months, just when humans are moving into the water to cool themselves down. Stingrays will gather in large numbers in hot weather, making for risky bathing.

RANGE: California

ZONE: subtidal to 70 ft

HABITATS: shallows; quiet bays; estuaries; sand and mud

LENGTH: to 22 in

COLOR: brown, gray; mottled yellowish markings

The upper surface of the Round Stingray is light brown or gray, with various mottled markings. These colors help it blend in with the seafloor, where it rests and moves about in search of its favorite foods, such as crabs, shrimps and various snails and clams. The young develop inside the female, and she gives birth to them in quiet bays and estuaries where they remain until they grow and mature.

White-cap Limpet
ACMAEA MITRA

The White-cap Limpet is frequently washed up on shores, where the strong surf pounds the shell to a dull white. Unlike other limpets, with their low profile, the shell of this limpet is very high compared to its length, giving it a pronounced cone-shaped appearance. The base is almost round, and the apex, or high point of the shell, is quite central. The shell is thick and the interior is a smooth white.

When alive, the White-cap Limpet is more likely to appear pink, because it is coated with Encrusting Coral (p.199) on which it feeds. Found on exposed, rocky shores, as well as protected, rocky areas, its high and prominent shell would be a disadvantage in rough surf, however, a powerful foot keeps it well adhered to the rock. Look out for this limpet at low tide, and do not confuse it with its smaller cousin, the Corded White Limpet (*A. funiculata*), which has ribs radiating from the central apex.

OTHER NAME: Dunce-cap Limpet

RANGE: Southern California to Alaska

ZONE: lower intertidal; subtidal to 100 ft

HABITATS: exposed and protected rocky shores

LENGTH: to 1.5 in

HEIGHT: to 1 in

COLOR: white shell, with pink growths

Fingered Limpet

LOTTIA DIGITALIS

When you clamber about on the rocks high up the beach, there are few animals to be noticed. Closely hugging rocks, the Fingered Limpet is one of the conspicuous mollusks that you'll find. This limpet's oval shell is colored gray-green and brown, with paler spots flecked here and there. Strong ribs radiate outwards from the apex (high point) of the shell, making the edge of the shell wavy. The slightly hooked apex is close to the front end of the shell.

This tolerant limpet enjoys the pounding surf, but avoids the baking sun of the upper intertidal zone where it grazes on algae. It prefers vertical surfaces facing the surf, and crevices offer a bit of protection. A powerful foot sucks firmly onto the rock—a great deal of force is needed to remove a limpet, so leave it alone because you risk damaging its shell. Empty limpet shells reveal a glossy white or pale blue interior, with a rich caramel-colored blotch at the high point. A black, wavy margin adds to the limpet's beauty.

OTHER NAMES: Ribbed Limpet; *Collisella digitalis*

RANGE: Southern California to Alaska

ZONE: upper intertidal; spray or splash

HABITATS: exposed, rocky shores

LENGTH: to 1.25 in

COLOR: gray-green, brown; white spots

SIMILAR SPECIES: Rough Limpet (p. 56)

File Limpet

LOTTIA LIMATULA

Tiny beads or scales compressed into fine ribs give this limpet its name. Its fine-woven texture will often give the creature a serrated edge, although the edge sometimes wears away. Tan to greenish-brown above, the File Limpet's interior is white, with a dark rim and a small, brown spot in the middle. The apex (high point) is set towards the front end of the shell, and the profile is very low, so that the limpet hugs the rocks closely.

The File Limpet is common in California, more so than at the northern end of its range in Puget Sound. It grazes on the microscopic algae covering the rocks, and each limpet has its own preferred feeding grounds that it likes to return to again and again.

OTHER NAME: *Collisella limatula*

RANGE: Southern California to Washington

ZONE: middle to lower intertidal

HABITATS: exposed and protected rocky shores

LENGTH: to 1.75 in

COLOR: tan to greenish-brown

Limpets will take on different proportions depending on where they choose to live. Study a large rock with limpets on both sides; you will notice how the limpets on the sheltered side grow taller and more elaborately than those on the wave-swept side, where a low profile is more important.

Rough Limpet
LOTTIA SCABRA

The common Rough Limpet closely resembles the Fingered Limpet. It has a variable shell in shades of brown, gray or green. The apex, or high point, of the shell is at the front end, and is not so pronounced as in the Fingered Limpet. Distinctive ribs radiate from the apex, making a heavily sculptured shell, and the ribs give the shell a scalloped or even saw-toothed margin. Older Rough Limpets appear to be heavily eroded and pale at the apex. The interior of the Rough Limpet is whitish, and has an irregular, brown blob at the apex. Along the scalloped margin is a series of dark spots, not unlike the Fingered Limpet but more coarsely defined.

This limpet becomes active at night or when it is submerged by a high tide. Once it has found a favorite location in which to rest, it will return to the same spot time after time. Eventually, by eroding the rock with its tongue, or radula, it leaves a precise scar, 'a home scar,' in the rock into which it neatly fits. Such a good fit, however, does little to deter the predatory attentions of the shorebirds and crabs that like to dine on Rough Limpets.

OTHER NAME: *Collisella scabra*
RANGE: California to Oregon
ZONE: middle to upper intertidal; spray or splash
HABITATS: rocky shores
LENGTH: to 1.25 in
COLOR: variable gray, green and brown
SIMILAR SPECIES: Fingered Limpet (p. 54)

Rough Keyhole Limpet

DIODORA ASPERA

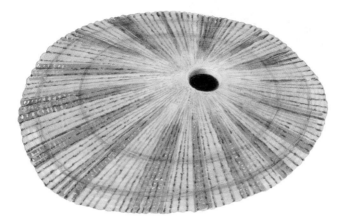

Rather like a volcano with a crater at its summit, this limpet is an attractive find at the low-tide line. The hole at the apex (high point) allows the Rough Keyhole Limpet to send a current of water over its gills, the water shooting out of the top. The oval base is often fringed with small 'teeth' because of the many fine ribs radiating from the apex. The color is variable, from gray to white, with dark gray or purple rays. The underside is plain white. The Volcano Limpet (*Fissurella volcano*) is very similar but much smaller, and the Great Keyhole Limpet (*Megathura crenulata*) also has a hole but grows to 4 inches in length.

RANGE: Southern California to Alaska

ZONE: lower intertidal; subtidal to 50 ft

HABITATS: rocky shores

LENGTH: to 2.75 in

COLOR: white or gray; with darker rays

Hidden away between the limpet's mantle and foot is the surprisingly large worm, *Arctonoe vittata*. This commensal relationship benefits both parties. The worm gets a protective home and reportedly, as a rental payment perhaps, will protect the limpet from marauding sea stars—the worm nips the feet of attacking sea stars to put them off. If this action fails, the limpet will extend its mantle over the rough shell, thus becoming slippery smooth and impossible for the sea stars to grasp.

Giant Owl Limpet
LOTTIA GIGANTEA

The largest of the North American limpets gets its name from the dark-colored attachment scar inside its shell, which is said to sometimes resemble the head of an owl. The interior of the shell is highly polished, and can come in shades of brown, blue and white. The shell has been used for making jewelry, because it can be so beautiful. The exterior is usually heavily eroded, but white flecks on a generally brown base can be seen along the margins of the shell. The limpet has a very low profile, tucked snugly against the rocks of exposed shores.

RANGE: Southern California to Washington
ZONE: middle intertidal
HABITATS: rocky shores
LENGTH: to 4.5 in
COLOR: brown flecked with white

Just like the Rough Limpet (p. 56), the Giant Owl Limpet etches out a 'home scar,' an eroded depression, that is usually in a clearly defined grazing territory. These are very noticeable when the territory is amongst dense mussel clumps. Look for bare patches of rock that are among the closely packed bivalves. The limpet keeps this area clean and grazes on the algae that colonize the patch. These territories are more evident in California, especially south of San Francisco, than in the northern limits of its range. In Central California the limpet grows larger and is more abundant.

Pacific Plate Limpet
TECTURA SCUTUM

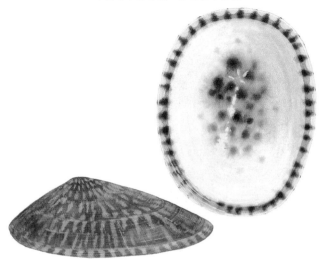

The Pacific Plate Limpet has a profile so low that it got named after dinnerware. Smoothly textured, the upper side is a gentle brown or green-brown, and beautifully marked with cream-colored lines radiating from the apex. Sometimes this limpet can be seen transporting a rooftop garden of algae, which gently wave in the current.

This limpet moves up and down with the tide, consuming microscopic and encrusting algae. It is nocturnal by nature, and huddles tightly against rocks by day. The smell of a starfish is enough to make this limpet break into a run, though remember that speed is all relative—a limpet running and panting still looks painfully slow.

OTHER NAME: *Notoacmaea scutum*

RANGE: Northern California to Alaska

ZONE: middle to lower intertidal; subtidal

HABITATS: rocky shores

LENGTH: to 2.5 in

COLOR: brown, green-brown; cream markings

Should it succumb to the starfish's pursuit, then the empty shell that is left is an attractive one to find. A glossy, white underside is bordered with an intermittent dark brown band, with additional splotches of brown in the middle. The similar Mask Limpet (*T. persona*) has a solid dark border, as well as distinctive and sometimes face-like markings inside, and the Shield Limpet (*L. pelta*) grows larger and has more prominent ribbing.

Onyx Slipper Shell

CREPIDULA ONYX

I n Central California, the beautiful Onyx Slipper Shell is one of the larger slipper shells. These are limpet-like snails stuck on rocks or other shells. The exterior is a dull brown color, but the interior comes in glossy shades of caramel and brown. The whitish shelf inside is the unusual feature that gives these shells their name. At one end of the oval shell is an apex that points off to one side, and from this several lines might radiate down the exterior.

RANGE: from Monterey Bay south

ZONE: low-tide line; subtidal to 300 ft

HABITATS: open coast; bays

LENGTH: to 2 in

COLOR: pale brown exterior; glossy brown interior

These strange mollusks often come in stacks, with older and larger females at the base and smaller males at the top. As they grow, the males will change their sex to female. Slipper shells do not move about like limpets, preferring to stay put and filter the water for tiny nutritious bits and pieces. In Northern California, a more likely slipper shell is the Pacific Half Slipper Shell (*Crepipatella dorsata*), which is smaller (1 inch) and lacks the rich colors of the Onyx Slipper Shell. To find out about the diminutive Slipper Snail (*Crepidula adunca*) refer to the Black Tegula (p. 76).

Black Abalone
HALIOTIS CRACHERODII

Abalones are prized by people and otters for their firm flesh. The dark-colored foot of this common abalone is a less popular food item than other varieties, such as the larger Red Abalone (*H. rufescens*) that shares the same range. However, even the Black Abalone can be hard to come by in the intertidal zone because many have been collected; it is seldom found north of Mendocino County. Sucked onto rocks like a limpet, the abalone grazes on a thin film of algae. Please do not remove it out of curiosity—the thin edge of the shell is damaged easily, leaving it vulnerable to predators such as starfish.

RANGE: Southern California to Oregon

ZONE: middle to lower intertidal; subtidal to 20 ft

HABITATS: rocky shores

LENGTH: to 6 in

COLOR: green or blue-black

The Black Abalone's oval shell is blue or greenish-black and, unlike its close relative the Japanese Abalone (*H. kamtschatkana*), the shell is seldom covered with a protective algal overcoat. The shell is thickened to one side and smooth in texture. The interior is pearly, and tinted with pinks and greens. The line of holes along the outer edge serves the same purpose as the hole of the Rough Keyhole Limpet (p. 57)—allowing a current of water to pass through the shell. Occasionally, the Black Abalone lacks these holes.

Frilled Dogwinkle
NUCELLA LAMELLOSA

The Frilled Dogwinkle, in shades of yellow, white and pale brown and sometimes banded, has decorations that are determined by its environment. If you are hunting for snails on the exposed coasts where the surf is strong, then look for smooth shells—it would be hard for a snail to look after frilly appendages in rough seas. Snails living in quieter waters don't have this worry; their frills can develop rather elaborately. This dogwinkle is found in crevices among rocks. Look under rocks near the low-tide line for clusters of yellowish eggs.

OTHER NAME: Wrinkled Purple

RANGE: Northern California to Alaska

ZONE: middle intertidal to shallow subtidal

HABITATS: rocky shores

LENGTH: to 4 in

COLOR: brown, yellowish; cream markings

The Frilled Dogwinkle is a carnivore, feasting on barnacles and mussels, clams and oysters. So effective and common is it that, in some regions, the lower spread of the Acorn Barnacle (p. 155) and the upper limit of mussels are determined by this snail's appetite. In turn, this gastropod is consumed by the Red Crab (p. 145). When threatened, or to hide from the weather and the sun when the tide is out, the snail withdraws into its shell and tightly closes the door, its operculum.

Emarginate Dogwinkle
NUCELLA EMARGINATA

Sometimes pretty, sometimes dull, this highly variable species is a resident of exposed, rocky shores, often in crevices near barnacle and mussel beds. It feeds on both of these, drilling a neat hole in the shell with its serrated tongue, or radula. Of the mussels, the Emarginate Dogwinkle prefers the Blue Mussel (p. 101), perhaps because the shell is thinner and requires less work to drill through. This dogwinkle also lives on shores that are slightly protected, but is absent from quiet water.

The shell is stubby, with a short spire, and its ribs are often white and set against a dark-colored base, usually giving a striped appearance. The Emarginate Dogwinkle can be yellow to dark brown and gray. The opening to the shell is tinted yellow, and if the snail is still inside, a dark brown operculum (door) will be tightly shut against you. The operculum also protects against water loss when the tide is out. Hermit crabs enjoy taking up residence in these small and manageable homes when the snail inside has died. Don't confuse the Emarginate Dogwinkle with the Angled Unicorn, which has a taller spire and prominent ridges.

OTHER NAME: Striped Dogwinkle

RANGE: Southern California to Alaska

ZONE: middle to lower intertidal

HABITATS: rocky shores

LENGTH: to 1 in

COLOR: variable, yellow, brown or gray; white stripes

SIMILAR SPECIES: Angled Unicorn (p. 64)

Angled Unicorn

ACANTHINA SPIRATA

A ngled Unicorns get their mystical name from a prominent spine or horn that sticks out from the lip of the aperture of the shell. Some people speculate that this 'horn' might be used to help tease open the Angled Unicorn's favorite prey of barnacles and bivalves, but actually the snail is armed with a drilling tongue, or radula. With this radula, it drills a small hole through the shell of its prey and then dines on the soft flesh in-side. Rocky areas in moderately protected waters are good places to find unicorns. Look among breakwaters and in bays, as well as under rocks in the middle intertidal zone, for groups of them huddled together.

OTHER NAME: Angular Thorn Drupe

RANGE: Southern California to Washington

ZONE: intertidal

HABITATS: stones; rocks; mussel beds of moderately protected waters

LENGTH: to 1.5 in

COLOR: dark gray, yellowish; brown lines

SIMILAR SPECIES: Emarginate Dogwinkle (p. 63)

The Angled Unicorn has pronounced ridges on each whorl of the shell, which pro-duce a tall, stepped spire. The base color is gray or yellowish, and lines revolving around the whorls are usually dark brown. These lines are crossed by pale ribs running the length of the shell, and can result in a checkered appearance. You might confuse the Angled Unicorn with the short-spired Emarginate Dogwinkle. If you are not sure, check for the unique horn of the unicorn shell.

Dire Whelk
SEARLISIA DIRA

The dismal gray version of this elegant snail might have inspired such an ominous name, but it does come in more attractive and variable shades of brown. The aperture, or opening, to the shell is a chocolate-brown, and the shell itself sometimes sports a pink or white coating of encrusting algae. The twisting spire is long, with many ribs that sculpt the lip of the aperture where the shell is quite thin.

The Dire Whelk is found on rocky shores and frequently in tidepools, which is certainly dire news for many of the other residents of those areas. This whelk is both scavenger and carnivore, and will feast on living limpets, chitons and other snails. Injured animals will have to suffer the attentions of the whelk as well, because it will start biting at any part of a creature that it can. The Dire Whelk will also exploit feeding starfish by chewing on the prey they are holding onto. Carrion will do just fine as well, the whelks homing in on anything they can smell— for which they have quite a talent

OTHER NAME: Spindle Whelk

RANGE: Central California to Alaska

ZONE: middle to lower intertidal

HABITATS: tidepools; rocky shores; open coasts; bays

LENGTH: to 2 in

COLOR: gray to brown

SIMILAR SPECIES: Lurid Rocksnail (p. 67)

Sculptured Rocksnail

OCENEBRA INTERFOSSA

This little carnivore comes in many shapes, but only grows to 0.75 inches. Some rocksnails have whorls that are very distinct and prominently ridged, whereas others, as illustrated, are smoother. Deep grooves are interspersed between the ribs. The color varies from gray to orange-brown, and the surface texture is usually a rough one. Barnacles, oysters and clams make up the Sculptured Rocksnail's diet. It drills a hole with its radula, a serrated tongue, and then proceeds to dine on the flesh inside. There's not much a barnacle can do about it, because it is firmly stuck to the rock and unable to run away from the rocksnail. Rocky shores and quieter waters are the domain of the Sculptured Rocksnail.

The Lurid Rocksnail occurs with the Sculptured Rocksnail, but has a smoother shell. The Atlantic Oyster Drill (*Urosalpinx cinerea*) is the same size, but with less ridging and is colored yellow-gray. Introduced from the East, the Oyster Drill is commonly found in the oyster farms of the Northwest, and gets little respect from the farmers.

OTHER NAMES: Carpenter's Dwarf Triton; *Ocinebrina interfossa*

RANGE: Southern California to Alaska

ZONE: middle to lower intertidal; subtidal to 20 ft

HABITATS: sheltered, rocky shores

LENGTH: to 0.75 in

COLOR: variable gray to orange-brown

SIMILAR SPECIES: Lurid Rocksnail (p. 67)

Lurid Rocksnail

OCENEBRA LURIDA

O nly growing to 1.5 inches, this mollusk is beautifully formed with well-rounded whorls. The Lurid
Rocksnail prefers rocky or gravelly shores near the
low-tide line or in subtidal waters. From Point Conception
south, this snail retreats into the subtidal zone, preferring
the cool of the water. Around the whorls are numerous ribs
that are variably pronounced from snail to snail. The pale
yellows, caramels and browns
are sometimes overlaid with
darker streaking. Barnacles are
the mainstay of this rocksnail's
diet, the snails drilling through
the tough shell of the crustaceans to consume them from
within their protective homes.
Some have been seen to rasp
away at the almighty Gumboot
Chiton (p. 102), which could
probably feed a rocksnail for
life!

OTHER NAMES: Lurid Dwarf
Triton; *Ocinebrina lurida*

RANGE: Southern California to
Alaska

ZONE: lower intertidal; subtidal
to 180 ft

HABITATS: rocky shores

LENGTH: to 1.5 in

COLOR: variable pale yellow,
brown

SIMILAR SPECIES: Dire Whelk
(p. 65), Sculptured Rocksnail
(p. 66)

From Monterey Bay south-
wards, the much smaller Circled
Rocksnail (*O. circumtexta*) is common where the surf is
strong. This cousin of the Lurid Rocksnail has coarser ribs
and a distinctive band or two in dark brown. The Lurid
Rocksnail might also be mistaken for the longer-spired Dire
Whelk, which can be grayer in coloration, or the Sculptured
Rocksnail, which has deeper grooves.

Joseph's Coat Amphissa

AMPHISSA VERSICOLOR

Small but strong, Joseph's Coat Amphissa is a more common find in the south of its range. Tidepools, with rocks and rubble, and near the low-tide line are a good place to hunt for this busy little snail. It is an active mollusk, and can be seen moving quickly about the rocks—quickly for a snail at least. Closer inspection of the shell can reveal that a tiny hermit crab has taken up residence. North of Sonoma County, you are more likely to come across the Wrinkled Amphissa (*A. columbiana*). This similar amphissa grows a bit larger. Both are aggressive little carnivores.

Joseph's Coat Amphissa is typically yellow or light brown, and is frequently mottled with pale and darker markings. Inside the aperture is a line of small, rounded teeth, although these teeth have nothing to do with biting. The vertical and horizontal ribs result in a gently beaded texture. This texture is similar to the Giant Western Nassa, which grows larger and more rounded, and the Eastern Mud Whelk, which is found on mudflats.

OTHER NAME: Variegate Amphissa

RANGE: Southern California to Washington

ZONE: lower intertidal; subtidal to 150 ft

HABITATS: rock; rubble; tidepools

LENGTH: to 0.75 in

COLOR: light brown or yellow; sometimes mottled

SIMILAR SPECIES: Giant Western Nassa (p. 70), Eastern Mud Whelk (p. 69)

Eastern Mud Whelk

ILYANASSA OBSOLETA

While cruising the mudflats of quiet bays, you are sure to be in the company of the Eastern Mud Whelk. This species was introduced from the Atlantic Coast, and it has set up successful homes in many of the bays of California, especially in San Francisco Bay. Look along the low-tide line for this snail. You will notice a myriad of trails left by worms, snails and other small invertebrates; some of these trails will be the tracks of the Eastern Mud Whelk, left in its quest for food. This mud whelk, like many whelks, is a scavenger, and it sniffs its way along and through the mud, siphon held high, in search of decaying matter. A dead fish will bring it out.

OTHER NAMES: Eastern Mud Nassa; *Nassarius obsoletus*
RANGE: California
ZONE: lower intertidal
HABITATS: quiet bays; mudflats
LENGTH: to 1.25 in
COLOR: brown, dark brown
SIMILAR SPECIES: Joseph's Coat Amphissa (p. 68), Giant Western Nassa (p. 70)

These are brown or dark brown snails, although sometimes they appear greenish, a coloration resulting from a thin film of algae growing on the shell. The tip of the spire is often eroded and cracked, and might even be partly missing. The shell resembles the Joseph's Coat Amphissa of rocky shores and the much larger and more beautiful Giant Western Nassa that shares this habitat.

Giant Western Nassa

NASSARIUS FOSSATUS

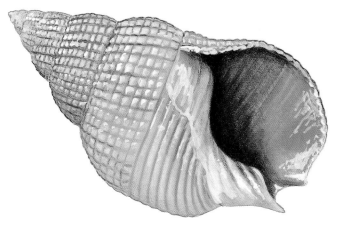

The finely sculptured Giant Western Nassa is the most common of the whelks, and is found in muddy sand where the water is quiet. Growing to 2 inches, it is a large shell that comes in shades of yellow, brown and gray, with a beaded surface texture. The aperture is wide, and a rich orange colors the inside. The shell is mostly glossy. The yellowish Western Fat Dog-whelk (*N. perpinguis*) is similar, growing to 1 inch in length and is found from Central California southwards.

OTHER NAMES: Channeled Dog Whelk; Channeled Basket Shell

RANGE: Southern California to British Columbia

ZONE: middle to lower intertidal; subtidal to 60 ft

HABITATS: sand and mudflats

LENGTH: to 2 in

COLOR: yellow, brown, gray

SIMILAR SPECIES: Joseph's Coat Amphissa (p. 68), Eastern Mud Whelk (p. 69)

The Giant Western Nassa prefers the fine sand and mud of bays because it is easier for this robust snail to shuffle its way through the particles. The whelk has a keen nose for decaying matter, and is an active scavenger of the low-tide line, as well as an occasional predator of other shellfish. It is fast moving, which perhaps allows it to get to the food before the many other organisms in this habitat. Don't expect to see Giant Western Nassas racing along the surface of the mud—they are usually buried just below the surface.

Leafy Thorn Purpura
CERATOSTOMA FOLIATUM

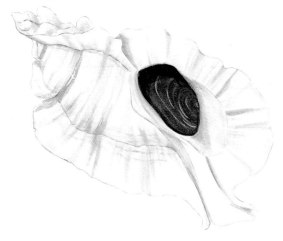

Finely frilled and delicately colored, this snail's beauty is sufficient to rival some of the more stunning tropical species. Three frills run vertically up the spire, and their elaborateness depends on where the snail lives. On the exposed coast where the snail tolerates surging currents, large frills would be a disadvantage. Where the water is calmer, the snail can grow frills to its heart's content. White in color, the shell is often adorned with attractive bands of reddish-brown, which is the same color as the horny operculum shutting the snail inside. Farther north, the snails show more darker coloration.

OTHER NAME: Leafy Hornmouth
RANGE: Central California to Alaska
ZONE: lower intertidal; subtidal to 200 ft
HABITATS: rocky shores; boulders; tidepools
LENGTH: to 3.5 in
COLOR: white, yellowish

The frills have an interesting function beyond looks. Fish dislodge snails so that when they fall, they land with the aperture facing up. Then the fish has easy access to the foot and a tasty morsel. This snail, however, has a much higher chance of landing the right way up; it is flicked by the currents that are generated by the frills as it falls. Barnacles and bivalves make up its diet, and in late winter it lays yellow egg-cases, frequently on its own shell.

California Horn Shell

CERITHIDEA CALIFORNICA

On mudflats and up salty creeks, the California Hornshell can be found in great numbers. They occur from Sonoma County southwards, and one of the best spots to see them in profusion is in Bolinas Lagoon, Marin County. Look among salt marshes and in tidal creeks for this tall-spired shell. It is usually dark brown, sometimes grayish, in color. Around the whorls there is sometimes a horny ridge, paler in color. This ridge marks the point when the snail was younger, and is the former lip to the aperture.

These gregarious snails feed on minute particles of decaying organic matter, or detritus, as well as tiny planktonic organisms left by the retreating tide. They are in turn fed on by fish and birds. This hornshell might be confused with the less common Mudflat Snail (*Batillaria attramentaria*) that is found in some regions of Northern California. These two can easily be told apart by the shape of the aperture, because the Mudflat Snail has a very round opening, while the California Horn Shell has an aperture that is much more elliptical.

RANGE: California

ZONE: intertidal

HABITATS: mudflats; estuaries; bays; salt marshes, especially tidal creeks

HEIGHT: to 1.75 in

COLOR: brown

Tinted Wentletrap
EPITONIUM TINCTUM

Exquisitely sculptured, the Tinted Wentletrap is a tiny treasure. Its unusual name comes from the Danish word for 'spiral staircase,' inspired by the 8 to 14 white ribs running the length of the shell. These ribs are offset against a gently colored shell tinted in brown and purple. The round aperture has a thick, white lip, and is closed by a horny operculum when the snail is alive.

These dainty snails rarely wander far from their food sources—the Aggregating and Giant Green anemones (pp. 138–139). Often buried in sand nearby, Tinted Wentletraps emerge to peck out chunks of the anemone's tentacles and foot. These snails gather in small groups, and when exposed by an ebb tide, burrow and conceal themselves in soft sand. If you notice a wentletrap moving about at speed and in an irregular fashion, you are more likely observing the antics of a hermit crab, the young of which are rather fond of these shells. The Money Wentletrap (*E. indianorum*) looks similar, but it is all white, is larger at 1.5 inches, and lives in deeper waters.

OTHER NAME: Painted Wentletrap

RANGE: Southern California to Alaska

ZONE: low-tide line; subtidal to 150 ft

HABITATS: near anemones

HEIGHT: to 0.6 in

COLOR: white; tinted with brown or purple; white ribs

Ringed Topshell
CALLIOSTOMA ANNULATUM

This ocean jewel is a rare treat of the intertidal zone, and it is found more commonly in the north of its range. Preferring to live in subtidal kelp forests, it can occasionally be found near shore. It is unique in that it has a yellow shell with a band of pink or purple and spirals of purplish beads winding their way round the sharply conical shell. The body of the snail, which is salmon-pink and flecked with brown, adds even more jazzy colors. Unfortunately, all these brilliant colors will fade a little when the mollusk dies.

OTHER NAME: Purple-ringed Topshell

RANGE: Southern California to Alaska

ZONE: lower intertidal; subtidal to 100 ft

HABITATS: kelp forests; rocky shores; open coast

HEIGHT: to 1.25 in

COLOR: pink-purple on yellow

This snail has omnivorous eating habits. Kelp makes up part of its diet, as does almost anything else that is growing on the kelp. On the seafloor, it pursues many of the smaller animals. When attacking, the Ringed Topshell rears up on its foot, spreading it wide, and then lunges at the target and traps it. Carrion makes good eating, too, and this snail has a keen nose for it.

Western Ribbed Topshell

CALLIOSTOMA LIGATUM

As tempting as a colorful candy, this beautiful topshell is caramel-brown and wrapped with tan spiral ridges, giving a striped appearance. Compared to other topshells, such as the flat-sided Ringed Topshell (p. 74), the Western Ribbed Topshell's appearance is chubby from the rounded whorls. Where the shell is older and worn, a delicate nacreous (pearly) blue shines through, giving this topshell its other name (see box). The muscular foot of the mollusk is black, with orange or creamy patches. This topshell is a potential find under rocks and in crevices of the intertidal zone along protected, rocky shores, but it is scarcer north of San Francisco Bay.

OTHER NAME: Blue Topsnail

RANGE: Central California to Alaska

ZONE: middle to lower intertical; subtidal to 100 ft

HABITATS: rocky shores

HEIGHT: to 1 in

COLOR: brown; tan stripes; blue when worn

Something of a non-fussy eater, this topshell will graze on kelp and algae, and quite enjoys the occasional sponge or tunicate. The sight or smell of a starfish is enough to send this snail running. If it is not fast enough, it will cover itself with a mucus coating. This slippery goo makes it rather difficult for the predatory starfish to grasp the Western Ribbed Topshell with its tube feet, and on a lucky day the snail might just slip out of its grasp.

Black Tegula
TEGULA FUNEBRALIS

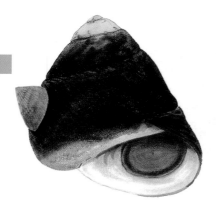

Abundant snails of the California coast, Black Tegulas enjoy the harsh upper intertidal reaches of rocky shores along open coasts. Smaller individuals tend to be higher up the shore than the larger individuals, and large aggregations collect in sheltered crevices when the tide is out. This tegula is a herbivore, grazing on the thin film of algae on rocks, as well as larger pieces of vegetable matter.

OTHER NAME: Black Turban

RANGE: Southern California to Alaska

ZONE: upper to lower intertidal

HABITATS: rocky shores; open coast

HEIGHT: to 1.75 in

COLOR: black, blue-black

Mostly black or blue-black, the summit of the spire erodes to reveal the shiny pearl surface beneath. Many tegulas will have a hitchhiker or two, including the Black Limpet (*Lottia asmi*) and the Slipper Snail (*Crepidula adunca*), which resembles a limpet. The Black Limpet grazes on algae on the shell's surface, and will hop onto a new ride when the snails collect together in a group. The Slipper Snail, with its hooked apex, just seems to enjoy the ride, filtering the water from on high. Red Crabs (p. 145) and Ochre Sea Stars (p. 123) love to dine on Black Tegulas.

Checkered Periwinkle

LITTORINA SCUTULATA

Several species of periwinkles litter the shores of California, and the Checkered is a likely find. It tolerates the upper intertidal zone, and when the tide retreats it can be found tucked into crevices and among algal holdfasts or mussel beds. For a creature that spends so much time exposed to the air, a tight-fitting operculum (door) is very important, shutting the snail away inside its shell so no moisture is lost. It drifts about the rocks grazing on microscopic or larger alga (including the Sea Lettuce, p. 192), and suffers from the hungry attentions of starfish, especially the Six-rayed Sea Star (p. 121).

RANGE: Southern California to Alaska

ZONE: upper to lower intertidal

HABITATS: rocky shores

LENGTH: to 0.5 in

COLOR: dark brown-black; white checkers

This small periwinkle has a darkly colored shell that is frequently flecked with pale markings, giving a checkered effect. The surface of the shell, unless eroded, is smooth and slightly glossy. You might mistake this periwinkle for the Eroded Periwinkle (*L. keenae*), which generally has more markings and lighter colors. The Eroded Periwinkle is so tolerant that it can be found even higher up than the Checkered Periwinkle, where the surf seldom sprays.

Purple Dwarf Olive

OLIVELLA BIPLICATA

A celebrated find among beachcombers, these snails are highly polished shells with variable and beautiful colors. The Purple Dwarf Olive is elongated and tapered at both ends, rather resembling the slippery olive fruits. The pointed ends and smooth surface help the snail burrow through the sand, while the large foot propels it along. By day they are concealed well below the surface, with perhaps just a slight dimple in the sand hinting at their presence. At night they are at the surface, the top of the shell often poking through.

Gray and purple are the dominant colors of the Purple Dwarf Olive, with brown stripes marking the suture of the short spire. The aperture is long, allowing the extensive foot to come out. A long siphon is used to suck water down from the surface. Purple Dwarf Olives gather in groups, perhaps as foraging parties, which certainly makes finding a mate easier in the vast expanses of sand. They sift the sand for decaying bits and pieces of organic material and occasionally take small prey. In turn these snails are the victims of the other common sand-resident, Lewis's Moonsnail (p. 82).

RANGE: Southern California to Alaska

ZONE: middle to lower intertidal; subtidal to 150 ft

HABITATS: sandy beaches and flats

LENGTH: to 1.25 in

COLOR: variable purple, brown, gray

Striped Barrel Snail
RICTAXIS PUNCTOCAELATUS

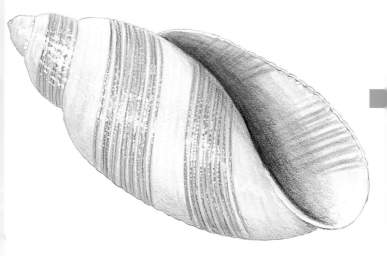

This delicate snail is a locally abundant resident of sand and mud flats, especially in Central California. Further north it is harder to come by, and is confined to deeper waters. Occasionally gathering in large numbers, they feed on tiny deposits left on the surface of the sand and mud. Striped Barrel Snails also turn up in sandy tidepools and between the roots of eelgrass plants.

The shell is delicate and appears bulbous, hence its delightful other name of Carpenter's Baby Bubble. The whitish shell is small, less than 1 inch in length, and is adorned with two broad bands of bluish-gray. On closer inspection, you will notice that these bands are each a collection of parallel lines. With a bubbly shape comes a very large aperture, or opening, to the shell. Through this aperture, the snail can squeeze its large, white foot up into the shell. Some snails possess an operculum, much like a door, with which they seal themselves in. The Striped Barrel Snail does not have an operculum with which to protect itself.

OTHER NAME: Carpenter's Baby Bubble

RANGE: Southern California to Alaska

ZONE: lower intertidal; subtidal to 300 ft

HABITATS: sandflats; tidepools; eelgrass beds

LENGTH: to 0.75 in

COLOR: white, with dark bands

California Cone
CONUS CALIFORNICUS

Small and plain, the California Cone is a somewhat dull relative of the exotic and beautifully marked tropical species of cones. The small shell is gently rounded and is usually colored in caramels, sometimes with an angled, paler band around the largest whorl of the shell. The short spire and comparatively huge main body whorl result in a long and thin aperture out of which the living animal emerges.

This shell is quite a common find south of San Francisco Bay, where rocks, gravel and sandy areas are its home. By day search under rocks, because this snail is active by night. It has a voracious appetite for a wide range of organisms, including another snails. When the California Cone finds an animal to its liking, it stabs it with a modified tongue, or radula, and injects poison that calms the prey. This snail proceeds to swallow the victim whole. Some of the tropical species of cone shells are notorious amongst collectors for their potentially dangerous stings, but this humble cone is of no concern.

RANGE: San Francisco Bay southwards

ZONE: low-tide line; subtidal to 100 ft

HABITATS: mixed rock, gravel and sandy areas

LENGTH: to 1.5 in

COLOR: pale brown

California Trivia
TRIVIA CALIFORNIANA

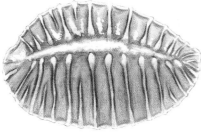

The attractive California Trivia can be found throughout much of the state. In shape it resembles and is related to the tropical and colorful cowries. This snail is purplish-brown in color (hence its other common name of Coffee Bean Shell), and has a pale stripe down the middle of the back. The upper side is rounded, while the underside is flat. Pale ribs curve round from the upper side to the lower, giving a toothed margin to the trivia's long, thin aperture. When living and active, the soft, fleshy mantle of the mollusk emerges and wraps over most of the upper surface of the shell, rather like an elaborate overcoat.

OTHER NAME: Coffee Bean Shell

RANGE: California

ZONE: low-tide line; subtidal to 250 ft

HABITATS: rocks; seaweeds; tunicates

LENGTH: to 0.5 in

COLOR: purplish-brown

Trivias feed on tunicates and other similar soft organisms. Thus, they will usually be found where their favorite food source is, as well as among rocks and seaweeds near the low-tide line and in subtidal waters. In Central and Southern California, the Appleseed Erato (*Erato vitellina*) can be found. This trivia is the same size, but lacks the white ribs and is a vivid purple color.

Lewis's Moonsnail
POLINICES LEWISII

O ne of our largest intertidal snails, the almost round Lewis's Moonsnail can be found on sandy flats. From the large aperture a most enormous foot emerges, and is seemingly too much to squeeze back into the shell. The beige foot almost covers the shell, and to tuck it all away, water must be squeezed out through tiny pores. The large, horny operculum (door) then seals it all in. The Moonsnail can't breathe when shut in, and would rather not do so for long.

RANGE: Southern California to Alaska

ZONE: lower intertidal; subtidal to 500 ft

HABITATS: sandy flats; bays; quiet waters

HEIGHT: to 5.5 in

COLOR: tan, brown

Burrowing through the sand, Lewis's Moonsnail particularly enjoys finding helpless clams stuck and buried where they thought they were protected. The Moonsnail wraps its foot around them and drills a hole with its radula. Once the contents are chewed out, the empty valves wash ashore with the distinctive hole, as shown on the Common Pacific Littleneck (p. 94). In turn, the Moonsnail is pursued by the Sunflower Star (p. 125) or occasionally by its own kind. The mystical sand collars of this snail are formed around the shell when mucus is secreted, with eggs inside. Sand quickly adheres to form a layered sandwich, 6 inches across, that washes ashore in summer.

Pacific Pink Scallop
CHLAMYS HASTATA HERICIA

Pretty in pink, this shell's beauty is often masked by an encrusting growth of camouflaging sponges. The upper valve is illustrated above—the paler, lower valve is pressed against the bottom. The rounded shells have a wavy margin, and darker growth rings in shades of pink and purple show clearly. Thin ribs are mixed with the more robust, and minute spines give a rough texture. South of Monterey Bay, the more spiny Pacific Spear Scallop (*C. h. hastata*) and the colorful Wide-eared Scallop (*Leptopecten latiauratus*) also occur.

OTHER NAME: Spiny Pink Scallop; Swimming Scallop

RANGE: Southern California to Alaska

ZONE: low-tide line; subtidal to 500 ft

HABITATS: rocky reefs; sandy beds; quieter waters

LENGTH: to 3.25 in

COLOR: white, yellow, pink, purple

SIMILAR SPECIES: Giant Rock Scallop (p. 85)

The arrival of a starfish is enough to send the Pink Scallop into a flapping frenzy, during which water is squished out of its shell to give some jet propulsion. When the scallop is living and agape, the water is being filtered for plankton, and a row of bright green eyes can be seen peeking out. More often you will come across this tasty morsel dead and on your plate, because it is a regular part of the commercial harvest. If you have been gathering them yourself, you would be wise to check with authorities about the levels of pollution in the area.

Clear Jewel Box
CHAMA ARCANA

The upper shells of the Clear Jewel Box are frequently washed up on shore. They are easily recognizable for the unusual leafy appendages adorning the outer surface of the shell, and their tough nature allows them to withstand the beating of the surf. The color is mostly white, but there is often a tinge of pink or orange, especially near the umbo. Inside, the shell is white. The shell has a translucent quality, hence its name of Clear Jewel Box. The left or lower valve will seldom be found cast up on the shore. These valves remain securely fastened to the rocks near the low-tide line or in subtidal waters. The lower valve is very thick and deeply dished.

This jewel box is seldom found north of San Francisco Bay, even though it can be found all the way up to Oregon. Another jewel box that shares the same range is the Reversed Jewel Box or Chama (*Pseudochama exogyra*). This one settles onto rocks with its right valve, and is rarely colored as beautifully as the Clear Jewel Box.

OTHER NAME: Agate Chama

RANGE: Southern California to Oregon

ZONE: lower intertidal; subtidal to 260 ft

HABITATS: rocky shores; gravel

LENGTH: to 3.5 in

COLOR: translucent white; pink or orange tint

Giant Rock Scallop
CRASSODOMA GIGANTEA

So tasty is this prized delicacy that it's the lucky naturalist who finds one intertidally. It is slow growing and lives up to 50 years, so think about the life you are removing if you want to harvest one. It can take up to 25 years to become full grown and quite a size it reaches, too. As a juvenile this scallop is free-swimming, and can be confused with the Pacific Pink Scallop. Pretty soon though, the scallop settles on a rock and sticks to it. Thereafter, the upper valve grows irregularly with the rock, and becomes encrusted with sponges, worms and anything else that thinks the scallop is a rock.

If observed alive, the flesh on the gaping shell is a brilliant orange, and small, blue eyes are lined along the gap. Empty upper shells frequently turn up on the shore in fragments, but are easily identified by a deep purple stain in the hinge area. Native peoples once used the shells for jewelry and ground up the burnt shells to make paints. No doubt they didn't let the colorful flesh go to waste either.

OTHER NAME: Purple-hinged Rock Scallop; *Hinnites giganteus*

RANGE: Southern California to Alaska

ZONE: lower intertidal; subtidal to 150 ft

HABITATS: rocky shores

LENGTH: to 10 in

COLOR: orange juvenile; encrusted adult

SIMILAR SPECIES: Pacific Pink Scallop (p. 83)

Pacific Shipworm
BANKIA SETACEA

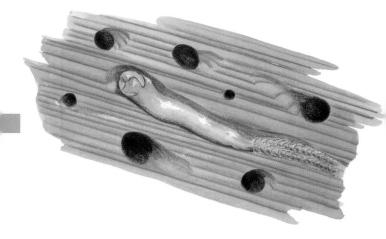

Feared by the wooden shipbuilders of the past, the Pacific Shipworm can destroy wooden structures with its burrowing antics. Not a worm at all, but a greatly extended bivalve, the shipworm has two sharply serrated shells that it twists to carve a home in the wood. These tiny shells are white, and the burrows are lined with a calcareous secretion. At the rear end are two odd feathery structures called 'pallets.' These tiered ornaments protect the two siphons that pump water in and out of the burrow, and serve as plugs for the entrance.

OTHER NAME: Feathery Shipworm

RANGE: Southern California to Alaska

ZONE: intertidal and subtidal

HABITATS: wood only

LENGTH: shell 0.25 in; body to 3.3 ft

COLOR: white shell

Young shipworms are free-swimming, soon settling on wood and burrowing into it. It is easier for them to follow the grain of the wood, and although a plank might be riddled with burrows, they never cross over each other. Digesting some of the wood, shipworms rely more on filtering the seawater through the burrow entrance, and extracting the planktonic wildlife. If you find some driftwood, try breaking it open to expose the mollusks within. If they have long since died, their shells and pallets might still be inside.

Bent-nosed Macoma

MACOMA NASUTA

The thin, white shells of the Bent-nosed Macoma have the unique habit of bending to one side. This habit is explained by the bivalve's preference for lying on its side and sending its siphons to the surface. Buried just 4 to 6 inches under the surface, the orange siphons extend upwards to sift for tasty sediments on the muddy sands. Once the clam has vacuumed up every morsel, it digs its way along to new territory and starts again.

The Bent-nosed Macoma is common in bays and quieter waters along the open coast. Being only a few inches below the surface, it often falls victim to the dreaded Lewis's Moonsnail (p. 82). Clams that have fallen victim to this snail bear the distinctive drilled hole. These dead shells frequently wash up on the shore; empty shells are plain white inside, much the same as the worn exterior. The Pointed Macoma (*M. inquinata*) is about the same size but is not bent to one side, much like the similar rounded Baltic Macoma (*M. balthica*).

OTHER NAME: Bent-nosed Clam

RANGE: Southern California to Alaska

ZONE: intertidal; subtidal to 150 ft

HABITATS: muddy sands of open bays; open coast

LENGTH: to 3 in

COLOR: mostly white

SIMILAR SPECIES: California Mactra (p. 89)

White Sand Macoma

MACOMA SECTA

Empty shells are commonly found on the surface, although the living bivalve is buried deep beneath the sand, as much as 18 inches under the surface. Despite being so far under, the long, white siphons still reach the surface. One siphon expels water while the other sucks it in, along with bits of debris vacuumed up from the seafloor. Living at such depths offers the clam the best protection.

OTHER NAME: Sand Clam

RANGE: Southern California to Alaska

ZONE: intertidal; subtidal to 165 ft

HABITATS: sand; quiet waters

LENGTH: to 4.5 in

COLOR: white

SIMILAR SPECIES: Bent-nosed Macoma (p. 87)

The shell of the White Sand Macoma is white, with a thin periostracum that adds hints of yellow and brown. Smoothly textured, this clam's left valve is flatter than the right, and there is no bending, as with the Bent-nosed Macoma with which this macoma might be confused. The interior is also white. Considered to be fine dining, the White Sand Macoma seeks its revenge in having a gut full of sand, so be warned—give the clam time to rinse out in clean seawater. Tiny pea crabs (*Pinnixa* sp.) often take up residence inside the clam where they have a safe home and a continual supply of food brought right to them—an easy life!

California Mactra

MACTROTOMA CALIFORNICA

O ne of the more common surf clams found cast ashore is the California Mactra. This unelaborate clam is white, and partially covered with a thin, brownish-gray periostracum. The small clam shell is quite thin and smooth, and the interior is also white. The California Mactra is buried in sand or muddy sand, most often in quiet water areas. Where it is locally abundant, it is gathered for the popular dish, clam chowder. North of Monterey Bay, this clam becomes scarce, and clam-hungry humans must direct their attentions elsewhere.

When this mactra's periostracum is worn away, as is often the case with shells that have been battered by waves for some time, the shell is all white. Bodega's Tellin (*Tellina bodegensis*) is a similar white bivalve with a shell that is more elongated and colored a very glossy white, a characteristic typical of tellins. Many surf clams, mactras, macomas, tellins and similar bivalves are cast ashore on sandy beaches after storms, and identifying them can present some challenges.

OTHER NAME: California Surf Clam; *Mactra californica*

RANGE: Central and Southern California

ZONE: intertidal; subtidal to 70 ft

HABITATS: sand; muddy sand; bays

LENGTH: to 2 in

COLOR: white, gray-brown

SIMILAR SPECIES: Bent-nosed Macoma (p. 87)

Common Washington Clam

SAXIDOMUS NUTTALLI

The Common Washington Clam is a rounded clam, with prominent concentric ridges The large oval shell is usually grayish on the outside and white inside. The outer surfaces are occasionally flecked with darker markings that are stains from iron sulfides. These are chemical compounds found in low-oxygen environments, such as the deep mud and sand where the clam likes to live. Bays and offshore waters far from rough surf are preferred. Large clams can be as much as 20 years old, and often host tiny pea crabs (*Pinnixa* sp.) inside their shells.

The range of this clam overlaps with its close relative, the Smooth Washington Clam (*S. gigantea*). This clam, as its name implies, is smoother, lacking the prominent ridges. The Smooth Washington Clam occupies the mud of Northern California and beyond, while the Common is found in mud and sand of central and southern regions of the state. In Central California their ranges overlap. Both are important contributors to the clam industry, especially the Smooth Washington Clam of the north. Regulations sensibly restrict the harvesting of these shellfish, ensuring that there will be clams for many years to come.

OTHER NAME: Butter Clam

RANGE: Central and Southern California

ZONE: low-tide line; subtidal to 150 ft

HABITATS: mud; sand; bays; offshore

LENGTH: to 4.75 in

COLOR: grayish

Soft-shell Clam

MYA ARENARIA

Despite being a common clam in bays and especially estuaries, the Soft-shell Clam is actually an introduced species from the Atlantic Ocean. First released in California, this clam has now made it all the way up to Alaska. It was probably a stowaway with deliberately introduced oysters late in the nineteenth century. Many people see this arrival as a blessing because of the clam's fine taste and quick-growing nature, and it has long been an important food source. These clams thrive in estuaries where the salinity is low, burying themselves in several inches of sand and mud. At low tide when you walk near them, they retract their long siphons, squirting water into the air.

OTHER NAME: Mud Clam

RANGE: Central California to Alaska

ZONE: intertidal; subtidal to 240 ft

HABITATS: estuaries; bays; mud and sand

LENGTH: to 5.5 in

COLOR: grayish and brown

The whitish shell has a thin and pale brown periostracum. Irregular ridges and growth lines mark the exterior, while the inside is smooth and white. The way the spoon-like addition to the hinge points up is unique to the Soft-shell Clam, but it only occurs on one of the two shells. Although the shell has recorded maximum length of 5 inches or more, it is hard to come by such fine specimens because they are heavily harvested.

Pacific Gaper
TRESUS NUTTALLII

This clam is one of the largest in California, weighing as much as 4 pounds. The lengthy siphons are so voluminous that it cannot withdraw them into the two valves. Thus, when dug up, the Pacific Gaper is most definitely gaping. If you are plodding about on sandflats, the clam retracts its fused siphons and shoots a jet of water into the air. Jump up and down, and you can really get them going! This white or yellowish clam is tucked as much as 3 feet under the surface and has a brown coating where the periostracum remains. To the north, in Oregon, the clam can easily be confused with the Fat Gaper (*T. capax*) that has a shell that is more oval and inflated.

OTHER NAMES: Summer Clam; Otter Clam; Horseneck Clam

RANGE: Southern California to Alaska

ZONE: low intertidal; subtidal to 100 ft

HABITATS: sandflats

LENGTH: to 9 in

COLOR: white, yellowish, brown

The flesh of harvested Pacific Gapers is popular among some shellfish aficionados, some of whom can be observed digging to great depths to obtain these chunky meals. At such depths, it is possible that the victim of this hunt will be the mighty Geoduck (*Panopea abrupta*). The similar, fleshy Geoduck has a more oblong shell, and supports a big clam industry in the Pacific Northwest.

Nuttall's Cockle

CLINOCARDIUM NUTTALLI

This shell is a delight to find, and if both valves are still joined at the hinge, when viewed from the ends they make a beautiful heart-shape. Strongly ribbed, the grayish shell is covered in a rich yellow to brown periostracum. The interior of the almost circular valves is a pale yellow-white. Well-defined ribs give a scalloped margin to the shell, and darker growth rings are evident. Much older Nuttall's Cockles have ribs that are worn down with age. Younger cockles might show some darker mottling on the shell.

The short siphons restrict the cockle from burrowing too deeply, and it often sits on or near the surface of muddy sands. To cope with this high-risk environment, the cockle has a muscular foot. When a hungry Sunflower Star (p. 125) gets too close, the cockle can flip and jump about, evading the star's grasping arms. Such strategies allow the cockle to live for up to 16 years. However, it is less adept at escaping commercial fishing—this cockle is a favorite for many.

OTHER NAMES: Basket Cockle; Heart Cockle

RANGE: Southern California to Alaska

ZONE: low intertidal; subtidal to 180 ft

HABITATS: mud; sand; gravel; quiet waters

LENGTH: to 5.5 in

COLOR: gray, brown, yellow-brown

Common Pacific Littleneck

PROTOTHACA STAMINEA

A poor digger, this Littleneck can be found in abundance in firm, muddy gravel. It has short siphons, for which it gets the Littleneck name, that confine it close to the surface, making harvesting easy for enthusiasts hungry for some cockle flesh. Unfortunately for these bivalves, small jets of seawater easily mark their location. If you are set on eating them, show some respect for the other organisms by using a small tool to extract your target. The minimum size harvestable is 1.5 inches, ensuring that the clam will not be over-harvested.

OTHER NAME: Native Littleneck; Rock Cockle; Steamer Clam

RANGE: Southern California to Alaska

ZONE: middle to lower intertidal; shallow subtidal

HABITATS: coarse sand; mud; gravel; quieter waters

LENGTH: to 3 in

COLOR: tinted white; brown markings

SIMILAR SPECIES: Japanese Littleneck (p. 95)

The finely textured surface results from the many radiating and concentric ridges formed by the ribs and growth lines. Usually whitish in color, there can be tints of yellow, and darker brown markings often take the form of zigzags. The shell is quite thick, but not thick enough to deter the predatory Lewis's Moonsnail (p. 82) from drilling a hole near the hinge and consuming the Littleneck. Victims of the Moonsnail wash up on the shore, so be sure to look for the telltale hole.

Japanese Littleneck
TAPES JAPONICA

This accidental introduction from Japan has been given so many different names that it must surely be suffering from an identity crisis. Smoothly textured and elegantly long compared to the Common Pacific Littleneck, this bivalve is found on a corner of the coast where few other bivalves are found—high in the intertidal zone. Now it has become quite common, especially in bays, ousting the native littleneck. Short siphons restrict it to the top 4 inches of mud, sand or gravel, and these littlenecks can easily be raked out.

With a base color of gray or brown, some Japanese Littlenecks are delicately marked with darker brown streaks or zigzags. The rear edge might be tinted in purple, and the smooth interior is mostly white tinted with yellow or purple. Favoring the middle to upper intertidal zone and not being buried very deep has its advantages and disadvantages—seldom does the bivalve fall prey to the Lewis's Moonsnail (p. 82); huge numbers, however, can be killed by cold winters in northern parts of its range.

OTHER NAMES: Manila Clam; Steamer Clam; *Venerupis philippinarum*

RANGE: Southern California to British Columbia

ZONE: upper intertidal

HABITATS: muddy sand; gravel; bays

LENGTH: to 3 in

COLOR: gray, brown; streaked

SIMILAR SPECIES: Common Pacific Littleneck (p. 94)

Pacific Razor Clam

SILIQUA PATULA

This bivalve is a true prize for beachcombers, and is more common in Northern California than Central. Buried just below the surface, its presence can be noted by a small dimple in the surface of the sand. Only the experienced hunter will be able to catch this swift bivalve—an uncovered razor clam can burrow out of sight in ten seconds! These clams make for fine dining if you can catch them, but bear in mind that they are also food for the flatfish and flounders that forage for them when the tide is in. Luckily for younger clams, they are protected from hungry human hunters; the minimum size allowed for harvesting is 4.5 inches.

OTHER NAME: Northern Razor Clam

RANGE: Central California to Alaska

ZONE: low-tide line; subtidal

HABITATS: sand; exposed beaches

LENGTH: to 7 in

COLOR: caramel, olive, cream

The long, thin shell is nicely polished and somewhat flattened. The periostracum, a tough outer coating on the shell, begins to wear away when it is pounded by the surf or scorched by the sun. As it peels off, it reveals a whitish shell beneath. The caramel or olive-green colors on the shell accentuate the growth rings quite clearly. On the inside the shells are pale, with a hint of pink or purple.

Punctate Pandora
PANDORA PUNCTATA

Pandoras are delicate shells, thin and almost translucent. They are usually subtidal, but will be found washed ashore from time to time. The Punctate Pandora is the largest of its kind to be found in California, growing to about 2 inches in length. It prefers sand and mud along the open coast. The shells are unusual in that they are curved into a crescent. They are pearly white inside and out, but on the inside tiny pits, like pinpricks, pockmark the surface.

One shell is mostly flat, while the other bends outwards, giving body to the bivalve. Look on this deeper shell for two roundish depressions; these are the attachment scars for the strong muscles that hold the bivalve together when it is alive. The concentric growth rings are faintly visible.

OTHEF NAMES: Dotted Pandora

RANGE: Southern California to British Columbia

ZONE: below low-tide line; subtidal to 165 ft

HABITATS: mud; sand; open coast

LENGTH: to 3 in

COLOF: pearly white

Other Pandoras found in California include the Threaded Pandora (*P. filosa*) that only grows to 1 inch, and does not bend in the same way as the Punctate Pandora. The Bilirate Pandora (*P. bilirata*) is even smaller. Both of these are found offshore, and are seldom found amongst the many shells cast ashore after storms.

False Pacific Jingle Shell

PODODESMUS CEPIO

These shells are said to jingle when rolling in the surf. They are distinctive shells commonly found on hard substrates, such as rocks and other shells. When a young jingle shell settles onto a suitable rock, the lower valve attaches to the rock. Through the hole of the lower valve, the mollusk sends strong filaments, or byssal threads, with which it holds onto the rock. The shell then grows into the shape of the rock to which it is attached. The whitish upper shell is complete and roughly circular. Algae growing in the shell can give the shell a greenish tinge. The interior is glossy. In the above illustration, look for the large, round muscle scar on the upper shell's interior. Put the two shells together, and the scar lines up with the hole of the lower shell. It is a strong muscle that keeps these shells attached to the rocks.

OTHER NAME: Abalone Jingle; Rock Oyster; Green False-Jingle

RANGE: Southern California to Alaska

ZONE: intertidal; subtidal to 300 ft

HABITATS: rocky shores

LENGTH: to 4 in

COLOR: whitish interior; greenish exterior

Two forms occur. North of Monterey Bay, the shell is thicker and more coarsely ribbed on the upper surface (and might go by the name of *P. macrochisma macrochisma*). South of Monterey Bay, the shell is thin and delicately marked (sometimes called *P. m. cepio*).

Native Pacific Oyster

OSTREA LURIDA

Once abundant along much of the coast, this oyster has shown sensitivity to pollutants. The Native Pacific Oyster has suffered from toxic pulp mill effluent, and attempts are now being made to reintroduce it into estuaries in Oregon. It shares parts of Northern California with the Giant Pacific Oyster (*Crassaotrea gigas*), which really is a giant, growing to as much as 12 inches. The Native Pacific Oyster only grows to 3.5 inches, but many consider it to have a superior taste.

The Native Pacific Oyster is found in many intertidal habitats, such as mudflats, gravel banks, tidepools, estuaries, rocks,

OTHER NAME: Olympia Oyster

RANGE: Southern California to Alaska

ZONE: low-tide line; subtidal to 165 ft

HABITATS: flats; tidepools; estuaries; firm substrates

LENGTH: to 3.5 in

COLOR: cream and gray; heavily marked

pilings and other shells. The valves grow rather irregularly, shaped by the substrate onto which they are attached, and no two shells will look the same. The exterior is cream to grayish, with white or darker markings, and there are visible but irregular growth rings. The interior is a smooth white, with green or blue tints. These oysters are rather indecisive about what sex to be and will switch from being female one year to male in the next.

California Mussel

MYTILUS CALIFORNIANUS

Large and unmistakable, this mussel thrives in the pounding surf of open coasts. Strong, protein-rich byssal threads extend from the foot of the mussel and cling tenaciously to the rock or to other mussels. Huge 'beds' frequently form in bands along the rocky shores.

One atop another, the unfortunate individuals at the bottom might have a hard time holding onto the rock, and large waves can tear out chunks of the bed. Once the rock is exposed again, new colonies will form.

The thick, beautiful shells are usually blue, with hints of brown. The tough periostracum that produces these colors can be seen peeling off the surface of dead shells. Low-profile ribs radiate out from the hinge of the shells. The interior is a glossy blue and white, and a few small but worthless pearls can be found. If mussels are a favorite for you, be warned that summer harvesting can be dangerous because the orange flesh accumulates the paralytic poisons from the notorious 'red tide.'

RANGE: Southern California to Alaska

ZONE: middle to lower intertidal; subtidal to 330 ft

HABITATS: rocks; pilings; exposed coasts

LENGTH: to 8 in; larger subtidally

COLOR: blue-black, brown

SIMILAR SPECIES: Blue Mussel (p. 101)

Blue Mussel
MYTILUS EDULIS

S maller than the California Mussel and less hardy, these delicate mussels are found in protected waters, often where there is low salinity (when fresh water mixes with seawater). Where conditions are right, the Blue Mussel can be seen growing along with the robust California Mussel. The Blue Mussel can form dense mats that make excellent habitats for many other organisms, which enjoy the shelter and protection between the shells. While brown shells are quite common, most of the long, elegant shells are blue-black. Blue Mussels lack the ribs and uneven texture of the California Mussel. The interior of their valves is blue-white. The Ribbed Mussel (*Ischadium demissum*) can sometimes be seen alongside. It is about the same size, but has fine ribs down its length.

OTHER NAME: Edible Mussel; Bay Mussel; *M. trossulus*

RANGE: Southern California to Alaska

ZONE: middle to lower intertidal; subtidal to 16 ft

HABITATS: quiet waters; rock; wood

LENGTH: to 4 in

COLOR: blue-black, brown

SIMILAR SPECIES: California Mussel (p. 100)

Attached to rocks and wood, especially pilings, these thin-shelled bivalves are a favorite food source for crabs, birds and starfish. The Blue Mussel's small size deters many a human hunter, and they avoid the predatory whelks of the open coast by living in quiet waters. As the gentle waves fall over them, the mussels take water into their shells where they filter it for tiny particles of food.

Gumboot Chiton

CRYPTOCHITON STELLERI

The giant of all chitons, this one is so large that it becomes easy not to notice, looking like a nondescript growth on a rock. While other chitons show the distinctive plates on their backs, the Gumboot Chiton has a girdle that completely covers it. Underneath are eight bony plates that sometimes wash ashore and have earned the name of 'butterfly shells' because of their shape.

OTHER NAME: Giant Pacific Chiton

RANGE: Southern California to Alaska

ZONE: lower intertidal; subtidal to 65 ft

HABITATS: rocky beaches

LENGTH: to 13 in

COLOR: reddish-brown

Most Gumboots are reddish-brown with a rough texture, and they are stuck to the rock with a large, muscular foot. Underneath, the foot is yellow. Gumboots are so large that they can be knocked off their footing by rough seas and might even turn up stranded on the beach. This chiton slowly creeps around grazing on encrusting and fleshy algae. Living for 20 years, this mass of flesh has surprisingly few predators, although the Lurid Rocksnail (p. 67) has been known to chew away at its surface, leaving little scars. Historically, it has been used as a food source by native peoples, but, unless you are fond of tough rubber, the Gumboot does not come recommended.

Black Katy Chiton
KATHARINA TUNICATA

The Black Katy Chiton is common on exposed coasts in the middle of the intertidal zone of northern regions, but is scarce south of Monterey Bay. This chiton is not sensitive to light, and will sit boldly atop exposed rocks. Other chitons tend to hide away. This primitive mollusk resembles a limpet with a large sucking foot, which holds on so tightly to the rock. The Black Katy Chiton moves about slowly grazing on algae.

The eight plates are visible on the back, but the shiny coal-black girdle covers most of each plate. The Black Katy Chiton adheres so well to rock that it can be hard to remove. If you are determined to study this animal further, use the blunt side of a blade to gently lift the animal off—it is easily injured. But if you can resist the temptation, then the chiton is sure to be happier. On the underside of the salmon-colored foot, the mouth can be seen at one end. In response to being removed from its snug rock, the chiton will begin to curl up to protect its soft underside.

OTHER NAME: Leather Chiton

RANGE: Central California to Alaska

ZONE: middle intertidal

HABITATS: rocky shores

LENGTH: to 5 in

COLOR: pale plates; black girdle

SIMILAR SPECIES: California Nuttall's Chiton (p. 107)

Merten's Chiton
LEPIDOZONA MERTENSII

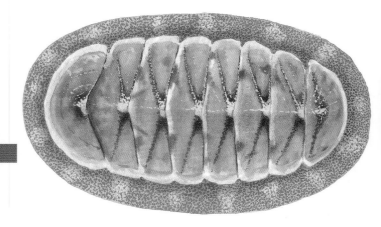

A little bit of searching is required to find these little ocean gems. Merten's Chiton is most often stuck to the underside of rocks in the intertidal zone, but it also lives in deeper water. When turning rocks in the hunt for this mollusk, be sure to replace them very carefully so as not to damage the chiton and the wealth of other creatures living there. Chitons are never in a hurry, and some will hang out in the same spot for many years—reportedly for as long as 25 years in some cases! Such persistent grazing on the same rock might result in an eroded depression underneath the chiton.

RANGE: Southern California to Alaska

ZONE: intertidal; subtidal to 300 ft

HABITATS: quiet waters; rock; wood

LENGTH: to 2 in

COLOR: variable browns, reds

SIMILAR SPECIES: Lined Chiton (p. 105)

This chiton is intricately marked and has a girdle surrounding the plates. The girdle, which is made from tiny scales in this chiton, is reddish-brown with paler patches that can appear as bands. The plates are very obvious and delicately marked in oranges, browns, reds and occasional white patches. Underneath, the foot runs for most of its length, and down either side of the foot are gills that allow this quiet creature to obtain oxygen from circulating water.

Lined Chiton
TONICELLA LINEATA

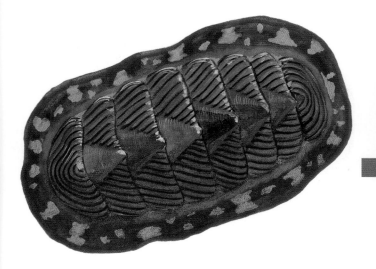

The Lined Chiton is the prize of the Pacific Coast and a feast for the eyes. Fortunately for us, it can be clearly and commonly visible on rocks exposed at low tide, although close attention is required to pick it out. The chiton is so heavily lined with many colors that it blends surprisingly well with its environment, often avoiding detection. When the surge channels are quiet, be sure to look along the walls, as well as near patches of pink encrusting algae. These jewels also turn up near the stunning Purple Sea Urchins (p. 131).

The patterns are highly variable and might involve just about every color of the rainbow. Most come reddish, with a smooth girdle blotched in creamy colors. The eight plates running down the back are busily lined in purple, black, white, pink, red, yellow and many other colors, depending on the individual chiton and where it has chosen to live. These chitons creep about the rocks consuming algae and anything growing on the algae, and are themselves the target of the Ochre Sea Star (p. 123).

RANGE: Southern California to Alaska

ZONE: lower intertidal; subtidal to 180 ft

HABITATS: rocky shores

LENGTH: to 2 in

COLOR: highly variable, mostly reddish

SIMILAR SPECIES: Merten's Chiton (p. 104)

Mossy Chiton
MOPALIA MUSCOSA

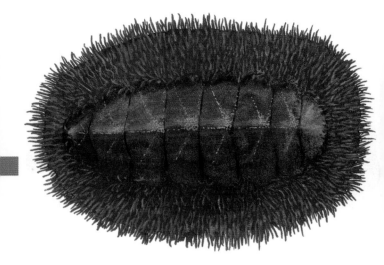

A thick, brown girdle covered in bristly hairs gives this chiton a mossy texture and appearance. The Mossy Chiton also comes in gray-green hues. The dark plates, exposed down the middle of its back, will sometimes have a pale line down the middle. This line is often obscured by an overgrowth of organisms that have made the chiton's back their home. Tubeworms, algae and barnacles are just some of the many organisms that you might find hitching a ride.

RANGE: Southern California to Alaska
ZONE: upper to lower intertidal
HABITATS: rocky shores; tide-pools; estuaries
LENGTH: to 3.5 in
COLOR: brown, gray-green

This species is a common chiton found between the tides on rocky shores. Its ability to tolerate low salinity allows it to venture into estuaries as well. The Mossy Chiton makes a home on a favorite patch of rock. It never roams too far, and after a night of foraging and scraping away for food on the surface of rocks, it will return to its favorite spot. The Hairy Mopalia (M. ciliata) is very similar, but has shorter bristles, and the Woody Chiton (M. lignosa) comes in similar dark brown shades but many other colors as well. The conspicuous Ochre Sea Star (p.123) makes a meal out of many different kinds of chitons.

California Nuttall's Chiton

NUTTALLINA CALIFORNICA

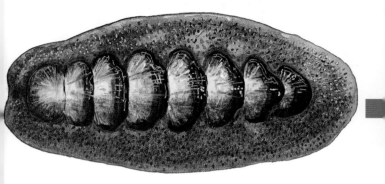

This darkly colored chiton often comes with a camouflaging overcoat of algae growing on its back. Some of these chitons lack this algae, and the plates down the middle of the back can be seen. When eroded, especially with older chitons, these plates appear pale, and the chiton might be confused with the Black Katy Chiton. However, the girdle surrounding the plates on the California Nuttall's Chiton is bristly, unlike the smooth girdle of the Black Katy Chiton.

This chiton doesn't move much. It will often have a home scar that it has worn away with its teeth. When the tide is out, the chiton returns to this little depression, and patiently waits for the tide to come back in and darkness to fall before roaming slowly about for Coralline Algae. It will also feed on bits of seaweed that settle near its patch. This chiton favors the upper intertidal zone of exposed coasts, and can often be found nestled in barnacle and mussel beds. Some of these chitons can live for as long as 20 years, always grazing the same patch of turf.

RANGE: Southern California to British Columbia

ZONE: upper to middle intertidal

HABITATS: barnacle and mussel beds; rocky shores; exposed coast

LENGTH: to 2 in

COLOR: dark brown, greenish

SIMILAR SPECIES: Black Katy Chiton (p.103)

Sea Lemon
ANISODORIS NOBILIS

Lemon in color, this nudibranch does indeed look like a piece of abandoned fruit. Some Sea Lemons come in stronger shades of orange, but all have scattered, black spots between the tiny tubercles that give them a rough texture. This sea slug is one of the largest sea slugs of the Pacific Coast, growing to 4 inches intertidally and to as much as 8 inches subtidally. Look for one tucked away under fronds of seaweed on rocky shores.

At the head end are two rhinophores, and at the rear is a plume of frilly gills fringed in white. The Sea Lemon is a hermaphrodite, each one being both male and female—which must surely make finding a partner easy! When provoked, this harmless-looking nudibranch emits a strong odor with fruity overtones, thought to dissuade any predator from consuming it. Sponges are the mainstays of the Sea Lemon's diet. Another sea lemon, the Monterey Doris (*Archidoris montereyensis*), is commonly found intertidally, but it does not grow so large and has black markings scattered up and between the tiny tubercles on the sea slug's back.

RANGE: Southern California to British Columbia

ZONE: intertidal; subtidal to 750 ft

HABITATS: rocky shores; under seaweed

LENGTH: to 8 in

COLOR: yellow, orange; dark spots

Yellow-edged Cadlina

CADLINA LUTEOMARGINATA

This whitish nudibranch is delicately fringed in bright yellow, and each tubercle on its back is tinged in yellow. Look under rocks and in tidepools near the low-tide line. The pale form of the Nanaimo Nudibranch (*Acanthodoris nanaimoensis*, which also comes in a dark phase) can be confused with the Yellow-edged Cadlina, but usually comes with tints of maroon on the gills at the rear and on the rhinophores. The reverse coloration, a yellowish body with white dots, occurs in the common White-spotted or Salted Doris (*Doriopsilla albopunctata*).

When gently touched, the surface of the sea slug feels very rough. This texture is created by tiny spicules that are derived from sponges, which use it in their skeletal matrix. The nudibranch eats the sponge and puts the spicules to good use, instead of excreting them. A spiky meal is much less appetizing to potential predators. Few creatures relish eating nudibranchs because they can smell bad, taste bad, feel too spiky, or are even armed with stinging cells. So, for the most part, nudibranchs can go about their business of eating uninterrupted.

RANGE: Southern California to Alaska

ZONE: lower intertidal; subtidal to 75 ft

HABITATS: rocky shores; under rocks; tidepools

LENGTH: to 3 in

COLOR: whitish; yellow markings

Ring-spotted Doris
DISCODORIS SANDIEGENSIS

This appealing nudibranch comes boldly marked with dark leopard-like spots and rings set against a creamy base color. It is commonly found along the Pacific Coast on the sides of boulders, under ledges and where seaweed can offer some protection. In the north of its range, the Ring-spotted Doris tends to have more rings, while in the south the rings can be so few in number that they seem completely lacking. Other Ring-spotted Dorises are dark instead of cream, especially in shades of chocolate-brown.

OTHER NAMES: Ringed Nudibranch; Leopard Nudibranch; *Diaulula sandiegensis*

RANGE: Southern California to Alaska

ZONE: lower intertidal; subtidal to 110 ft

HABITATS: rocky shores; crevices; seaweed

LENGTH: to 3.5 in

COLOR: cream to brown; dark spots

As with many nudibranchs, sponges are a favored food item, especially the encrusting Purple Sponge (p. 177). A rasping radula, inside the mouth on the underside of the slug, is used to bite away at the sponge. Tiny, hairy projections on the skin give a rough feeling to this mollusk, and the tuft of gills at the rear can be retracted inside. Each Ring-spotted Doris is both male and female, and after mating with another individual, the sea slug lays a curly ribbon of white eggs in protected nooks.

Opalescent Nudibranch

HERMISSENDA CRASSICORNIS

This flamboyant sea slug graces the entire Pacific Coast, and it is one of the commonest nudibranchs to be found. A slender, elegant body has many hair-like projections (cerata) in bands down each side of the body. The foot is translucent and lined with white or blue.

The cerata are beautifully and variably presented, with white, orange and brown markings—the brown is an extension of digestive glands from the gut. Most distinctive is the vivid orange line down the middle of the back; the rest of the colors and markings can be quite variable.

Tidepools on rocky shores, mudflats and beds of Eelgrass (p. 201) that are near the low-tide line are all the haunts of this aggressive carnivore. These nudibranchs readily consume small anemones, bryozoans, sea squirts, worms and much more. Opalescent Nudibranchs are even fond of taking a bite out of each other, perhaps in defense of a favorite feeding territory. When they consume prey with stinging cells, such as sea anemones, they store up the stinging cells in the ends of their cerata to aid in their own defense.

OTHER NAMES: Long-horned Nudibranch; Hermissenda; *Phidiana crassicornis*

RANGE: Southern California to British Columbia

ZONE: lower intertidal; subtidal to 110 ft

HABITATS: rocky shores; tidepools; eelgrass beds

LENGTH: to 3 in

COLOR: variable, pale with orange markings

SIMILAR SPECIES: Elegant Aeolid (p. 113), Pugnacious Aeolid (p. 116)

Sea Clown Nudibranch

TRIOPHA CATALINAE

Dazzling and comical, the Sea Clown Nudibranch can be seen in the tidepools of rocky shores. So bright and cheerful, it is hard to miss. The whitish body is covered in stubby protuberances, each of which is tipped in strong orange. The sensory rhinophores (tentacles) and the frilled ring of gills are also colorfully tipped. The head is broad and bears several branched and forward-pointing projections.

These sea slugs are most often about 1 inch in length, but can grow to an impressive 6 inches. Unlike many other nudibranchs with their tough and hardened skins, these ones are rather squishy and flimsy, and one would imagine that they would make delectable eating. However, these noticeable slugs are never touched, happily cruising about the tidepool unharmed—the brilliant orange might serve as a deterrent and warning that they don't taste good. Many nudibranchs, in calm pools, have the talent of walking upside-down along the undersurface of the water. This ability saves having to deal with all the obstacles of a trip along the bottom. Touch them gently and they will rapidly sink.

RANGE: Southern California to Alaska

ZONE: intertidal; subtidal to 110 ft

HABITATS: rocky shores; tidepools; kelp

LENGTH: to 6 in

COLOR: orange flecks on white

Elegant Aeolid
CORYPHELLA IODINEA

Few creatures come more beautiful than the Elegant Aeolid. Although it has a wide distribution up the Pacific Coast, the further north you go, the less likely you are to see this treasure. In rocky areas look along the low-tide line among kelp. Pilings are an excellent site for watching all kinds of marine life, and these feathery mollusks show up here, too. The nudibranch feeds on tunicates like Sea Pork (p. 179), as well as hydroids. If disturbed or anxious, the Elegant Aeolid will launch into open water and swim away with quick bends of its long, slender body.

OTHER NAME: *Flabellinopsis iodinea*

RANGE: Southern California to British Columbia

ZONE: low-tide line; subtidal to 110 ft

HABITATS: rocks; kelp; pilings

LENGTH: to 3.5 in

COLOR: purple and orange

SIMILAR SPECIES: Opalescent Nudibranch (p. 111), Pugnacious Aeolid (p. 116)

This nudibranch has a bright purple body adorned with vivid orange, finger-like growths, called cerata, rising from its back. Close inspection of each of these fingers will reveal a dark brown line inside, which is an extension of the gut. Few animals can be confused with this nudibranch, except the Opalescent Nudibranch with its bright and variable colors. Compare the Elegant Aeolid with the Pugnacious Aeolid and Opalescent Nudibranch, because they have a similar body plan.

Hopkin's Rose

HOPKINSIA ROSACEA

Few beachcombers will forget the first time they meet the petite and pretty-in-pink Hopkin's Rose. This elaborate little find, barely an inch long, is strikingly colored, and with its long, wavy projections, it is no wonder that it got named after a flower. Although it can be found all the way up into Oregon, this nudibranch becomes scarce north of Monterey Bay. Look along rocky shores and in tidepools near the low-tide line. At first sight, it might easily be mistaken for an anemone.

RANGE: Southern California to Oregon

ZONE: lower intertidal; subtidal to 18 ft

HABITATS: rocky shores; on or near Rosy Bryozoans

LENGTH: to 1.25 in

COLOR: pink

Pink is most definitely the color of the day for this nudibranch. It is pink all over, has a small ring of gills at the rear end that are dark pink, and it feeds on the pinkish Rosy Bryozoan (p. 174). Staying true to form, it even lays ribbons of pink eggs. The small, oval body is almost covered by the fleshy projections. However, these projections are not cerata, as they are with the Elegant Aeolid, because they do not have an extension of the gut inside. The small ring of darker-colored gills at the rear helps this sea slug extract oxygen from the seawater.

Navanax
NAVANAX INERMIS

A full-grown Navanax is a disturbing sight to other slugs and snails. This sea slug is a predator with an appetite. Once it has caught a sniff of the mucus trail of another mollusk, it pursues it at speed, and then swallows it whole. The Navanax haunts the mudflats and eelgrass beds of quiet waters. Mollusks of Northern California can rest easy, because the Navanax can only be seen from Monterey Bay southwards. Search the calm waters near the low-tide line when the tide is out, but remember when the tide turns, it races in at great speed over these flats.

The Navanax is a large sea slug, growing to an impressive 8 inches in length. The long body can be as much 2 inches wide, and is edged with wing-like extensions of the mantle. These extensions are fringed in bright orange or sometimes blue. Other splashes of electric blue are streaked and dotted on the dark velvety body. Like the neon lights of a city street, a host of bright colors line and dot the surface of this elaborate creature.

OTHER NAME: *Chelidonura inermis*
RANGE: Central and Southern California
ZONE: near low-tide line; subtidal to 25 ft
HABITATS: mudflats; eelgrass beds; quiet waters
LENGTH: to 8 in
COLOR: dark base; bright-colored streaks

Pugnacious Aeolid
PHIDIANA PUGNAX

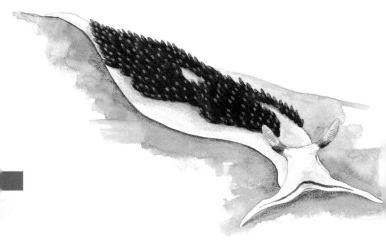

Several of the Californian nudibranchs are, without a doubt, some of the most beautiful sea creatures to be found. What they lack in size, they make up for in bright colors. One such nudibranch is the feisty Pugnacious Nudibranch, found more commonly in Central and Southern California. This 2-inch long sea slug gets its pugnacious name from its aggressive attitude. When put into confinement with another sea slug, it quickly attacks it. This little fighter is carnivorous, preying on anemones and many other soft-bodied, sessile organisms that are unable to flee.

OTHER NAME: *Phidiana hiltoni*

RANGE: California

ZONE: middle to lower intertidal; subtidal to 700 ft

HABITATS: rocky shores

LENGTH: to 2 in

COLOR: whitish foot; reddish cerata

SIMILAR SPECIES: Opalescent Nudibranch (p. 111), Elegant Aeolid (p. 113)

The Pugnacious Aeolid has a translucent body and a whitish margin along the edge of the foot. Most distinctive, however, are the many short cerata down its back. These are deeply colored in reddish-pink, and have a darker core. On the tip of each projection is a gold or yellowish dot. As if with bright lipstick, the face of the aeolid has a line of red stretching between the two antennae. Be sure to compare this aeolid with the similarly designed Elegant Aeolid and Opalescent Nudibranch.

Stubby Squid
ROSSIA PACIFICA

The attractive Stubby Squid is one of the best reasons to go down to the tidepools at night with a flashlight. Sometimes found in large tidepools, but more usually in subtidal zones, this squid has beautiful swimming control. Water is propelled out of the mantle cavity, shooting the squid backwards, and a small fin around the edge of the mantle provides subtle control.

A cluster of grabbing tentacles, for seizing fish and shrimp, surrounds the beak-like mouth. This squid will often sit on the bottom with its arms over its head. To help it blend in further with its environment, the speckles on its skin can change color very quickly. This talent is shared by many squid, and it is remarkable to watch. Small pigment patches are contracted or expanded to change the color density. The Stubby Squid is shorter and, well, stubbier than the sleek, common Opalescent Squid (*Loligo opalescens*). The Opalescent Squid is the market squid, and produces the 6-inch long egg-cases that wash ashore in summer and fall, and resemble pale jelly sausages. Peek inside and you might make out the tiny squid embryos.

RANGE: Southern California to Alaska

ZONE: lower intertidal; subtidal to 1200 ft

HABITATS: tidepools; inshore waters

LENGTH: to 5 in

COLOR: variable, often red

Red Octopus
OCTOPUS RUBESCENS

Persistent searching of large tidepools and surf grass at the low-tide line might reveal this fabulous mollusk. Advanced well beyond its snail relatives, this creature is highly intelligent and somewhat shy. However, don't inter- fere with it because it can still inflict a bit of a nip. The Red Octopus is a small octopus, with arms up to 18 inches long— small fry compared to the Giant Pacific Octopus (*O. dofleini*) with its arm-spread of 20 feet! The Giant Pacific Octopus prefers cold water, and it is an unlikely find in the intertidal zone of California.

RANGE: Central and Northern California

ZONE: lower intertidal; subtidal

HABITATS: rocky shores; surf grass

LENGTH: arm spread to 18 in

COLOR: reddish

At the base of the eight arms is a powerful beak-like mouth used to hack crabs, snails and a lot of other prey apart. Stalking and lunging are its preferred tactics for ambush, and seldom can the target escape the suction of the cups on the arm. Like the Stubby Squid (p. 117), the Red Octopus is gifted at changing its color to blend in with its home. A pile of empty shells and chunks of crabs reveal the den of an octopus.

Leather Star
DERMASTERIAS IMBRICATA

To some it smells of garlic, to others it has overtones of exploded gunpowder. Either way, the touch of the Leather Star is enough to make some species of anemone release their tenacious foothold on a rock and swim for safety. This starfish is a predator of anemones, urchins and cucumbers of the marine type. The mouth is in the middle of the underside, and rows of small tube feet on the underside of each arm help the animal move. Its name derives from the smooth and slippery skin on the upper surface, which gives it a leathery texture.

The Leather Star has five short arms and a robust build, but it is not as stocky as the variably colored Bat Star. The intricate patterns are usually made up of red or orange patches set against a blue-gray background. They are most often encountered in the low intertidal zone among rocks and occasionally in sandy areas. Protected bays are preferred, and pilings or sea walls can be good places to hunt for them. They sometimes turn up in tidepools.

RANGE: Southern California to Alaska

ZONE: lower intertidal; subtidal to 300 ft

HABITATS: rocks; sheltered bays; sea walls; pilings

DIAMETER: to 8 in

COLOR: red on blue-gray

SIMILAR SPECIES: Bat Star (p. 122)

Troschel's Sea Star

EVASTERIAS TROSCHELII

This elegant sea star inhabits the rocks and soft-bottomed shores of the protected coasts. To the south, it becomes increasingly rare. It is frequently confused with the Ochre Sea Star, despite some obvious differences between the two. Troschel's Sea Star has five rays that are more slender and a small central disk. It also comes in a whole range of colors from green to blue-gray, but most often in shades of red and orange. On the tip of each arm of the sea star is a small, reddish eye that has simple vision. Off to one side of the central disk is a small, round plate through which water passes in and out.

Troschel's Sea Star often turns up with the Ochre Sea Star near the low-tide line, especially in mussel beds and tidepools. Closer inspection reveals many tiny, whitish spines that do not form any patterns as they do with the Ochre Sea Star. The smaller and similar Pacific Henricia (*Henricia leviuscula*) grows to 7 inches, is less spiny, and also has five arms. Mussels, barnacles and limpets are eaten by Troschel's Sea Star.

RANGE: Central California to Alaska

ZONE: lower intertidal; subtidal to 230 ft

HABITATS: rocks; soft bottoms; protected waters; tidepools; mussel beds

DIAMETER: to 22 in

COLOR: highly variable, red to blue-gray

SIMILAR SPECIES: Ochre Sea Star (p. 123)

Six-rayed Sea Star

LEPTASTERIAS HEXACTIS

This small sea star comes in shades of green to black, orange and tan, and is occasionally mottled, too. Rather inconspicuous because of its often drab colors, this sea star requires some effort to find—look under loose rocks and boulders on the protected and open coast. The Six-rayed Sea Star is distinct for having six rays, instead of the more normal five, and a feathery-looking texture from closely packed spines.

OTHER NAME: Brooding Star

RANGE: Southern California to British Columbia

ZONE: middle to lower inter-tidal; shallow subtidal

HABITATS: rocky shores; under rocks; tidepools; mussel beds

DIAMETER: to 3.5 in

COLOR: highly variable, black to mottled tan

This sea star gets its other common name, Brooding Star, from the female's unusual winter behavior. Standing on the tips of her rays, she carefully tends a mass of yellowish eggs in the cavity for over a month, until they hatch. She then guards the tiny young until she feels confident that the baby stars can cling to the rocks on their own. After nearly two months, she can finally start to look for food and eat again. This sea star eats mollusks—including the exquisite Lined Chiton (p. 105)—and barnacles, and scavenges on the occasional dead meat drifting its way.

Bat Star
ASTERINA MINIATA

Wonderfully geometric with five stout arms, or rays, this sea star is locally abundant in parts of Northern California, but its distribution can be somewhat scattered. Where it is common, its bright colors make it conspicuous against rocks and in tidepools. Once in awhile the Bat Star will have more than five arms, sometimes as many as nine. It gets its name from its webbed arms, likened to a bat's wing. The commonest shades include bright reds and oranges, as well as darker shades of green, brown and even purple, with mottling in some.

OTHER NAME: Sea Bat; *Patiria miniata*

RANGE: Southern California to British Columbia

ZONE: lower intertidal; subtidal to 950 ft

HABITATS: rocks; tidepools; open coasts

DIAMETER: to 8 in

COLOR: highly variable, red, green, brown, purple, mottled

SIMILAR SPECIES: Leather Star (p. 119)

A Bat Star is not a fussy eater, happy to dine on almost anything. This sea star extrudes its stomach out of its mouth and wraps it around the food of its choice, digesting externally before swallowing. Algae and kelp are frequently consumed, but small animals do just as well. On the Bat Star's underside, look for the small, brown Bat Star Worm (*Ophiodromus pugettensis*) living in the grooves. The Leather Star is occasionally mistaken for the Bat Star—note that it has distinctive patterns, a smooth texture and slightly longer arms.

Ochre Sea Star

PISASTER OCHRACEUS

The striking orange form of this sea star is a common sight on exposed, rocky shores. Clinging to wave-swept rocks, these rough-skinned sea stars are also dark brown or purple; blunt, white spines give the coarse texture to the skin. A clean appearance is maintained by tiny pincers that peck and pull apart anything that lands on them. The sight or smell of this sea star is enough to send many intertidal organisms running, crawling, slithering or jumping for their lives.

Mussel and barnacle beds are the Ochre Sea Star's favorite domain—the appetite and abundance of which determine the lower limit of mussel beds. With its tube feet, the sea star gradually pulls the shells apart, inserts its stomach and slowly digests the contents—all of which can take a couple of days! These beauties are the sad victims of human ignorance. So hard and colorful are they that people take them home as beach souvenirs thinking they will dry up and look great on the mantle piece. Instead, they rot and smell terrible, so please leave them where they belong.

OTHER NAME: Pacific Sea Star; Purple Sea Star

RANGE: Southern California to Alaska

ZONE: intertidal; subtidal to 300 ft

HABITATS: exposed, rocky shores

DIAMETER: to 14 in

COLOR: orange-ochre, brown or purple

SIMILAR SPECIES: Troschel's Sea Star (p. 120), Giant Sea Star (p. 124)

Giant Sea Star
PISASTER GIGANTEUS

Close to the low-tide line, among rocks and sand, you might well catch a glimpse of the huge and chunky Giant Sea Star. Subtidally, this tough creature can grow to as much as 2 feet across, but is likely to be smaller (in the order of 8 inches) when found intertidally. A smaller Giant Sea Star might be confused with the more commonly found Ochre Sea Star, but they are easy to tell apart. The Giant Sea Star always has white, evenly spread-out spines that do not form patterns in the same way as they do in the Ochre Sea Star. Each white spine is surrounded by a blue halo, a feature absent in Ochre Sea Stars. Giant Sea Stars come in base colors of brown, tan, reddish or sometimes purplish hues.

RANGE: Southern California to British Columbia

ZONE: low-tide line; shallow subtidal

HABITATS: rocky shores; sandy areas

DIAMETER: to 24 in

COLOR: variable, with white spots circled with blue

SIMILAR SPECIES: Ochre Sea Star (p. 123)

Look for the Giant Sea Star in surge channels when the tide is out, where they might have come in on a feeding foray. But remember what dangerous places these channels can be when the tide is in. Giant Sea Stars prefer to dine on mussels, but will readily take other snails and bivalves, too.

Sunflower Star
PYCNOPODIA HELIANTHOIDES

The largest sea star in the world graces our western shores, and it is a spectacle worth looking for, but it does become scarcer in central regions. This sea star is subtidal, venturing into intertidal waters to forage, and occasionally getting stranded in pools as the tide goes out. Some have been measured at up to a staggering 40 inches across, though most are smaller. When young they have six arms, but as they age new arms are added until there are more than 20.

RANGE: Southern California to Alaska

ZONE: lower intertidal; subtidal to 1450 ft

HABITATS: rocky shores; soft bottoms; pilings

DIAMETER: to 40 in

COLOR: variable orange, red, brown or purple

These orange, brown or purplish sea stars are soft in appearance, gentle to the touch and brittle when handled—arms readily break off, so don't pick them up, just watch! They are rapid movers, at least when compared to other sea stars. The arrival of this giant in a tidepool is enough to send just about every organism nearby into a major panic, and the exodus begins. Purple Sea Urchins (p. 131) are a favored food, and their clean 'tests'—skeletons—can be plentiful, symbols of the ransack preceding your arrival. Just about every creature is eaten, including other species of sea stars.

Stimpson's Sun Star

SOLASTER STIMPSONI

Seldom seen but notable for its outstanding good looks is the Stimpson's Sun Star. Beachcombers occasionally come across this geometric delight at the low-tide line along rocky shores from Monterey Bay and northwards. It can grow as much as 20 inches across and live to the depths of 2000 feet. This sun star usually comes with ten arms in orange or red, and marked with a blue-gray stripe that runs down from the central disk to the tip of each arm. It doesn't have any spines, but it still has a rough texture.

RANGE: Central California to Alaska

ZONE: low intertidal; subtidal to 2000 ft

HABITATS: rocky shores

DIAMETER: to 20 in

COLOR: orange, red; with blue-gray stripes

Stimpson's Sun Star glides about on its many arms in search of sea cucumbers and tunicates to feed on, although it is itself a victim of the predatory attentions of Dawson's Sun Star (*S. dawsoni*). Dawson's Sun Star is a large sea star that is usually reddish, and resembles a cross between an inflated Stimpson's Sun Star and the Sunflower Star (p. 125). It has in the order of 13 arms, and enjoys pursuing sea stars its own size or larger, like the massive Sunflower Star

Esmark's Brittle Star

OPHIOPLOCUS ESMARKI

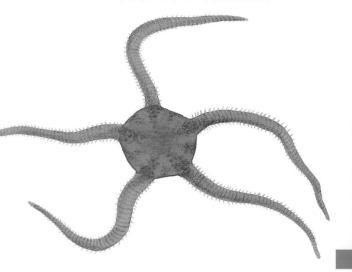

Brittle stars get their name from how easily they lose their arms when handled. This lost arm then regrows. However, the Esmark's Brittle Star is a lot sturdier than its name suggests. Normally, it has five arms radiating from a central disk that is quite large when compared to the proportions of other brittle stars. The spines are short, and the creature moves quite slowly—another unusual feature for a brittle star because many of them are quite capable wrigglers.

These brownish stars can frequently be found tucked under rocks or in small crevices, but only expect to turn up one of these brittle stars from Sonoma County southwards—they are absent in the rest of Northern California. While turning over rocks, you might well come across some common brittle stars like the Burrowing Brittle Star (*Amphiodia occidentalis*), with its smaller disk and greatly elongated arms. These arms really do break off easily, so give them a chance and don't mess with them too much. The brittle star might be more grateful if you just observed!

OTHER NAME: Smooth Brittle Star

RANGE: from Sonoma County southwards

ZONE: low-tide line; subtidal to 220 ft

HABITATS: soft bottoms; under rocks

DIAMETER: to 6 in

COLOR: brown

Spiny Brittle Star

OPHIOTHRIX SPICULATA

This unmistakable brittle star is a common sight along the coast of California. Look among the rocks when the tide is out, in tidepools and in submerged crevices. Dense clumps of algae, especially in the holdfasts, and invertebrates are also favored locations for the Spiny Brittle Star. Here, it can firmly clasp its surroundings with some of its arms, while letting the others sway about in the currents, filtering the seawater for food.

RANGE: California

ZONE: lower intertidal; subtidal to 6600 ft

HABITATS: rocky and soft-bottomed shores; tidepools; holdfasts; invertebrate beds

DIAMETER: to 15 in

COLOR: variable orange, tan, brown or green

The Spiny Brittle Star has five arms that are densely covered with long spines. The margin of the central disk is also fringed in spines. Each vicious-looking spine is itself covered in minute spinelets. The color is very variable, but is often orange and tan, with mottling. This brittle star also comes in various shades of green and brown. Whatever the color, it can always be recognized by the mass of spines. In deeper water, out of reach of the beachcomber, these brittle stars are known to gather by the million or more, which must be something of a creepy sight! Even inshore, where conditions are right, they will gather in big groups to feed.

Eccentric Sand Dollar

DENDRASTER EXCENTRICUS

A popular souvenir of beachcombers, the flattened Sand Dollar is commonly found on sandy beaches. The familiar gray or white dollar represents the skeleton, or 'test,' of the urchin, which usually lives just below the low-tide line in sandy-bottomed areas. When living, the test is covered with tiny spines that give it a dark brown or purple color.

Crowds of Sand Dollars can sometimes be seen vertically lodged in the sand filtering tiny particles from the water currents. Tiny hairs move the trapped particles towards the mouth.

In rough weather or at low tide, the Sand Dollar uses movable spines to bury itself further into the sand and flatten down

OTHER NAME: Sand Cookie

RANGE: Southern California to Alaska

ZONE: low-tide line; subtidal to 130 ft

HABITATS: sandy areas; sheltered bays

DIAMETER: to 3.25 in

COLOR: gray-white test; dark spines

so as not to expose itself to strong currents. Despite this activity, some will still end up stranded on the shore after a heavy storm. Here, they die and the spines are gradually washed away, revealing the characteristic five-petaled flower etched on the test, and hinting at the Sand Dollar's ancestral connection to sea stars. This off-centre pattern marks where the tube feet once emerged.

Red Sea Urchin

STRONGYLOCENTROTUS FRANCISCANUS

Vibrant in color, the Red Sea Urchin, the giant of the West Coast urchins, has spines growing up to 3 inches long. This formidable-looking armory not only serves to protect, but also snares drifting fragments of algae. The algae are then gradually pulled apart and eaten. These scavengers eat all kinds of food, including dead fish, and they are found on open and sheltered rocky shores.

RANGE: Southern California to Alaska

ZONE: low-tide line; subtidal to 300 ft

HABITATS: rocky shores; open and protected coasts

DIAMETER: to 5 in without spires

COLOR: pink, red, reddish-purple

During the lowest tides along calm shores, wander down to the water and you might be fortunate enough to witness stunning carpets of the Red Sea Urchin.

Sea Otters (p. 32) are fond of urchins, and they can be seen pulling them apart on their bellies while floating on their backs. Where otters flourish, Red Sea Urchins do not. People who have developed a fascination for eating these sea urchins' ovaries are additional threats to them. Between the spines are tiny, pincer-like projections that pinch away at anything venturing too close. These can be enough—but not always—to scare off the hungry attentions of Sunflower Stars (p. 125), but are certainly no good against humans.

Purple Sea Urchin
STRONGYLOCENTROTUS PURPURATUS

Gorgeously colored in purple, this vibrant urchin is a resident of the exposed, rocky coasts where the surf pounds. The Purple Sea Urchin is found in tidepools, and there is something of a mystery surrounding this relative of sea stars and cucumbers. Perhaps with their five teeth, maybe with their sharp spines, many Purple Sea Urchins end up in deep depressions in impossibly hard rock. It appears that they erode holes into the rock, and sometimes can never get out of them. Occasionally, they occur in such large numbers that the rock can be riddled with their burrows.

Algae are the main component of their diet, although it is likely that rock is also consumed (not that it has great nutritional value). Senior urchins, sometimes as old as 30 years, enjoy the exposed rocks, while the juveniles tend to hide away in small crevices or mussel beds. Young urchins that are less than 1 inch wide have greenish spines. Remarkably, the soft and squishy Sunflower Star (p. 125) can tolerate the urchin's spiny defense and will readily make a meal out of a Purple Sea Urchin.

RANGE: Southern California to Alaska

ZONE: middle to lower intertidal; subtidal to 30 ft

HABITATS: exposed, rocky shores; tidepools

DIAMETER: to 3.5 in without spines

COLOR: purple

Red Sea Cucumber
CUCUMARIA MINIATA

Sea cucumbers are definitely one of the more extraordinary features of the intertidal zone. Somewhat resembling a salad item, they are most definitely animal, and are related to starfishes and sea urchins. The Red Sea Cucumber has five rows of tube feet down its length, hinting at the shared ancestry—think of the Bat Star's (p. 122) five arms and the Eccentric Sand Dollar's (p. 129) five-lobed markings. These cucumbers can be hard to come by in Northern California.

When feeding, a fabulous display of ten crimson, branching tentacles opens up around the mouth. These tentacles filter the seawater for tiny particles of food. Once a tentacle is sufficiently loaded, it is drawn into the mouth and wiped clean. If hassled by enthusiastic beachcombers, the sea cucumber's tentacles retract and the whole body stiffens up. Often, the tentacles are all you can see of the buried cucumber. The conspicuous reddish California Stichopus has distinctive spines on its body, and in Monterey Bay the tiny, red Dwarf Sea Cucumber (*Lissothuria nutriens*) barely reaches an inch in length.

RANGE: Northern California to Alaska

ZONE: lower intertidal; subtidal to 80 ft

HABITATS: rocky shores; crevices

LENGTH: to 10 in

WIDTH: 1 in

COLOR: tentacles crimson; body red to purple

SIMILAR SPECIES: California Stichopus (p. 133)

California Stichopus

PARASTICHOPUS CALIFORNIENSIS

S quishy when fully extended, this clumsy-looking character can possibly be found near the low-tide line of protected, rocky coasts. It comes in shades of brown, red or yellow, and is covered in stout, pointed, spiny projections. Rows of tube feet are on the underside. Low tidepools and rock crevices are good places to look, but the California Stichopus has become scarcer owing to possible overfishing— the muscles of the sea cucumber have recently become an attractive commodity on which people dine.

Pale tentacles surrounding the mouth sift through detritus on the seafloor for any nutritious bits and pieces. A victim of the Sunflower Star (p. 125), the California Stichopus tries to avoid its predator—the smell of the sea star sets the cucumber into a rapid walk, like an inchworm's, or it can even swim away with undulations of its body. Failing this, the cucumber will eject its body organs through its mouth, abandoning them presumably so that the predator will dine on them. The cucumber will scurry away and grow new organs.

OTHER NAME: Giant Sea Cucumber; *Parastichopus californicus*

RANGE: Southern California to British Columbia

ZONE: low-tide line; subtidal to 300 ft

HABITATS: rocks; crevices; pilings; protected coasts

LENGTH: to 16 in

WIDTH: to 2 in

COLOR: variable brown, red, orange, yellow

SIMILAR SPECIES: Red Sea Cucumber (p. 132)

White Sea Cucumber

EUPENCTATA QUINQUESEMITA

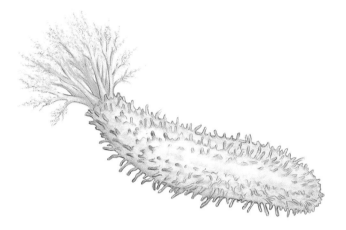

Long and slender, very much like the cucumber it is named after, this White Sea Cucumber is the most likely one of its kind to be found in Northern and Central California. It is small, so close inspection is required when trying to find it. The 4-inch long body is mostly white, sometimes tinted with faint colors. When the tide is out and during daylight hours, the sea cucumber's tentacles are withdrawn; as the sea cucumber is submerged, the yellowish tentacles emerge to filter the seawater for tiny particles of food. There are ten tentacles. When a tentacle is sufficiently loaded up with food, it is folded into the mouth and wiped clean.

Lines of tube feet run down the length of the body, helping the White Sea Cucumber move slowly about from crevice to crevice, among rocks and dense patches of seaweed and invertebrates. Look along the lower intertidal zone for this creature. Sometimes hanging over the edge of wharves in harbors can provide hours of entertainment—look at the pilings for a really busy perspective of the marine world.

OTHER NAME: Stiff-footed Sea Cucumber
RANGE: Southern California to Alaska
ZONE: intertidal; subtidal to 60 ft
HABITATS: pilings; rocks; crevices; rocky shores
LENGTH: to 4 in
WIDTH: 0.5 in
COLOR: whitish

Purple-striped Pelagia

PELAGIA COLORATA

A number of jelly-like blobs will be stranded on the beach or get caught in a tidepool by the receding tide. Graceful in the open ocean, it becomes quite amorphous and helpless when plumped on the sand by a large wave. One striking arrival on beaches, and occasionally in tidepools, is the huge Purple-striped Pelagia, with a bell 30 inches or more wide and deep purple lines and dots. The tentacles hang from the fringe of the bell and have stinging cells called 'nematocysts,' which are used to catch prey. Steer clear of these nematocysts, because they are very toxic. This jellyfish moves inshore in late fall and winter.

OTHER NAME: Purple-banded Jellyfish
RANGE: California
ZONE: inshore; offshore
HABITATS: stranded on beaches
BELL DIAMETER: to 32 in
COLOR: translucent white and purple

Other jellyfish that are tossed ashore include the Moon Jelly (*Aurelia aurita*). This jelly has a translucent bell, with four horseshoe-shaped organs in the middle of the bell, which is only 15 inches across. Sometimes clouds of these jellyfish drift close to shore, and are washed up in great numbers. The similar-sized Sea Nettle (*Chrysaora melanaster*) is also frequently stranded here, and has pale brownish markings on the bell and dark-colored tentacles.

Beroe's Comb Jelly

BEROE CUCUMIS

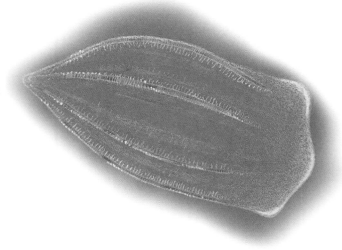

An infrequent gem stranded on the shore is Beroe's Comb Jelly. Although it appears at first sight to be just another blob of jelly, close inspection reveals some delicate beauty. The lines on the body refract light in pastel shades. When free-swimming, this creature gives off its own mysterious light. This comb jelly is flattened, tapered at one end, and has a broad front end. The huge mouth stretches right across the front, and is large enough for the comb jelly to swallow soft-bodied cnidarians, as well as crustaceans.

RANGE: Southern California to Alaska

ZONE: inshore

HABITATS: bays; stranded on beach

LENGTH: to 4.5 in

COLOR: translucent

The eight 'combs' running down the length of the body help propel the animal along, and give this group their common name. Another common comb jelly to wash up on shore is the Sea Gooseberry (*Pleurobrachia bachei*). These comb jellies turn up in large numbers on some beaches, and look like beads of jelly. A closer look will reveal the eight combs on the body. These small jellies do not sting, so be sure to pick them up and put them in a bucket. This way you can marvel at their delicate natures, and perhaps see them glow in the dark.

By-the-wind Sailor
VELELLA VELELLA

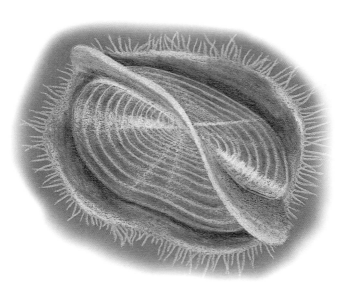

In spring the beaches might be littered with the 4-inch long hard skeletons of the By-the-wind Sailor. This bluish and translucent object is the remnant of a cnidarian that once sailed the ocean. The unusual structure cast ashore is filled with gas chambers that allow the animal to float at the surface. The vertical crest acts like a sail, and is set at an angle to the length of the body. This angled sail allows the sailor to tack against the wind, which works very well when the wind blows from the north, but when it shifts to the west more, the By-the-wind Sailor is driven ashore, sometimes in large numbers. Westerly winds usually happen in spring.

RANGE: California
ZONE: inshore; offshore
HABITATS: sea surface; stranded on beach
LENGTH: to 4 in
COLOR: bluish, translucent

Newly beached animals still have their fleshy parts, which include a ring of tentacles that are used to feed on small organisms swimming in the sea. After a few days all the soft tissue has decomposed, and all that remains is the horny and unique skeleton of the By-the-wind Sailor. After strong winds, these remains can be piled up in banks along beaches.

Aggregating Anemone

ANTHOPLEURA ELEGANTISSIMA

Aggregating Anemones can be seen in profusion throughout much of the intertidal zone, whether smothering rocks in tidepools or on isolated rocks on beaches. To find them on surf-pounded beaches, look on the sheltered side of rocks that are protected from beating waves. When exposed, the elegant blue or pink stinging tentacles are withdrawn, and the anemones appear as greenish blobs of jelly. Sand and gravel often adhere to the bodies of anemones in such quantities that the anemones seemingly disappear.

A large aggregation, or colony, is formed by one anemone that has repeatedly divided, or cloned. Two colonies beside each other will have a small gap dividing them, as if they are intolerant of touching each other. When solitary, this anemone can reach much larger sizes. The greenish color in the body of the anemone comes from tiny algae that are living in the host's soft tissues. They have a safe haven here, and are thought to provide some nutrition in return. Otherwise, the anemone depends on crustaceans or other small organisms that fail to escape the menacing armored tentacles.

OTHER NAME: Elegant Anemone

RANGE: Southern California to Alaska

ZONE: upper to lower intertidal

HABITATS: rocky shores; tidepools

DIAMETER: to 2 in closed; 3.5 in open

COLOR: green body; variable tentacles

Giant Green Anemone

ANTHOPLEURA XANTHOGRAMMICA

The stunning green form of this huge anemone is hard to miss on open, rocky coasts. Shining away in tidepools and surge channels, this anemone enjoys a rough ride from the waves. Its brilliance comes from a colony of algae growing inside the translucent flesh; here, the algae are provided with a home and offer some nutrition in return. If deprived of light, the algae can die, and the anemone loses its magnificent color. Look on the side of the dark column and foot for tiny Stearn's Sea Spiders (p. 172) quietly sucking away.

RANGE: Southern California to Alaska

ZONE: lower intertidal; subtidal to 50 ft

HABITATS: rocky shores; tidepools; surge channels

DIAMETER: to 10 in

COLOR: variable greenish-blue

The tentacles are armed with tiny cells that each have a miniature harpoon. If you brush your hand across the tentacles, they feel sticky—this sensation is the tiny harpoons trying to drag you in. Once some prey is caught, the tentacles pass it into the mouth in the middle, and the food is then digested. Anything that is not usable is then ejected out of the same hole. These anemones are often positioned where they can catch mussels that have been dislodged by rough surf.

Proliferating Anemone

EPIACTIS PROLIFERA

Petite and pretty, these delicate anemones come in a variety of colors in variable shades of red, green and brown. In rocky situations they tend to be pink or red, while on Eelgrass (p. 201) or algae they are green or brown. White stripes radiate from the Proliferating Anemone's mouth and mark the column. This anemone can often be found in small gatherings in tidepools and at the base of rocks usually along the open coasts and in bays. It is widespread along much of the Pacific Coast.

The odd breeding behavior of this anemone is worth noting. Eggs are fertilized inside the cavity, and then the tiny young move out of the mouth, slide down the side of the anemone, and settle down on the wide column. Here, the young will stay until they are large enough to fend for themselves. They don't wander too far, staying close to the parent and forming large patches of individual anemones. This squat anemone is eaten by the Leather Star (p. 119) as well as nudibranchs.

OTHER NAME: Brooding Anemone

RANGE: Southern California to Alaska

ZONE: upper to lower intertidal; subtidal to 30 ft

HABITATS: rocky shores; tidepools; eelgrass beds; seaweeds

DIAMETER: to 2 in

COLOR: variable green, red, brown, pink

Frilled Anemone
METRIDIUM SENILE

At low tide, in quiet waters, be sure to peek into pools or along pilings and seawalls for the beautiful Frilled Anemone. It does occur intertidally, but in quiet corners or under ledges. Calm seas are preferred and subtidally they can grow to enormous sizes. The anemone has a mass of thin, cream-colored tentacles, with a richly colored column that is often reddish-brown. The bushy tentacles are used to sweep up tiny floating sea life.

The Frilled Anemone has several ways of going about reproducing. Aside from using an egg and fertilizing it with the male's sperm, the anemone can split down the middle lengthways to create two identical individuals. Even more bizarre is its habit of leaving bits of its foot behind—each one of those bits can generate into a new anemone. The whiff of food is often the primary motive for making an anemone shift from its footing. When wandering around, this anemone defends its own space, readily shooting stinging cells at other anemones, which retaliate.

OTHER NAME: Plumed Anemone

RANGE: Southern California to Alaska

ZONE: low-tide line; subtidal to 100 ft

HABITATS: rocky shores; pilings; tidepools

HEIGHT: to 18 in

COLOR: variable reddish, brown, white

Painted Urticina
URTICINA CRASSICORNIS

A lovely name for a beautiful anemone, the Painted Urticina is a rarity hidden away in protected locations near the low-tide line. It is more abundant in the north of its range. This anemone commonly comes in shades of red and cream. Approximately 100 or so tentacles are banded, and deep-colored stripes run between the bases of the tentacles. The stout column and foot are sometimes uniformly colored, but usually come blotched with shades of red, cream and green.

OTHER NAME: Northern Red Anemone; *Tealia crassicornis*

RANGE: Southern California to Alaska

ZONE: lower intertidal; subtidal to 100 ft

DIAMETER: to 6 in

HABITATS: rocky shores; tidepools

HEIGHT: to 5 in

COLOR: variable red, green, cream

This anemone shows up in tidepools, and might be buried in the sand or gravel so that only the stunning crown of tentacles can be seen. This ring of waving projections is seen as certain death by small crabs, sea urchins, snails and some small fish—all of these are heartily enjoyed by the Painted Urticina. Once the prey succumbs to the will of the anemone, it is transferred to the central mouth and down into the body cavity, which serves as one huge stomach. Sometimes you can even see large prey being forced inside the body, doubtlessly to last the hungry anemone some considerable length of time!

Club-tipped Anemone

CORYNACTIS CALIFORNICA

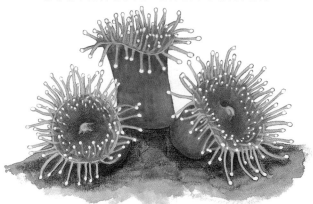

The Club-tipped Anemone is one of the prettiest anemones to be found in the low intertidal zone of California's open coastline and bays. It is small, about an inch big, and is most often in red or pinkish shades. Each tentacle is swollen at the end and is often paler in color, and with these whitish dots on red, this anemone has earned its other name of Strawberry Anemone. Club-tipped Anemone also comes in shades of orange, purple or a ghostly white. Look among rocks, under ledges and on pilings for colonies of this creature.

The swollen tentacles contain the largest stinging cells of any anemone, but they are not harmful to us. A colony of these anemones, with their extended tentacles, however, is lethal to the small organisms that swim by. These colonies are made by the Club-tipped Anemone's remarkable ability to repeatedly divide, or split, down the middle—an easy way to reproduce. This anemone is, in fact, more closely related to Orange Cup Coral (p. 144) than to the other anemones described in this book.

OTHER NAME: Strawberry Anemone

RANGE: California

ZONE: low intertidal; subtidal to 150 ft

HABITATS: open coast; bays; rocky shores; tidepools; pilings

HEIGHT: to 1.25 in

DIAMETER: to 1 in

COLOR: red, pink, purple, orange, white

Orange Cup Coral
BALANOPHYLLIA ELEGANS

The closest thing we have to the incredible coral reefs of the tropics is this tiny cup coral. The Pacific waters are too rough and cold to support anything more exciting in this region, and intertidally, this coral is the only one we will see. A little work is required to find it, because it often prefers the darker overhangs of ledges that are very close to the low-tide line. Here, it is not at risk of drying out, because it is protected from direct sunlight and uncovered for only a short time.

RANGE: Southern California to Alaska

ZONE: lower intertidal; subtidal to 160 ft

HABITATS: tidepools; crevices; overhangs; surge channels; open coast

DIAMETER: coral cup to 0.4 in

COLOR: orange

The Orange Cup Coral, when exposed at low tide, looks like a sharp and calcareous cup, with radiating walls inside and a tint of orange. In tidepools the delicate, translucent creature emerges from its stony home, spreading its faintly orange tentacles to catch and sting small prey. This coral is related to sea anemones, differing in that it builds a solid coral base to withdraw into. Other cup corals can be found at greater depths, but well out of reach of the beachcomber.

144

Red Crab

CANCER PRODUCTUS

When lifting rocks at low tide, you might well be amazed to see the stunning, deeply colored Red Crab. This crab is commonly found from quiet bays to exposed coasts. Distinctive features include the rounded 'teeth' bordering the edge of its wide carapace and the black tips to its pincers. If these pincers don't put you off, gently have a look at the crab's underside for the soft creamy yellow color. Keep in mind that the pincers are strong enough to crack through a shell!

A very similar Pacific Rock Crab (*C. antennarius*) has red speckles on its underside. The Oregon Cancer Crab (*C. oregonensis*) is a much smaller crab that might be confused with young Red Crabs. Juvenile Red Crabs are a treat to find, because they are variably colored from red to white, blue to orange, with a carapace frequently etched with elaborate markings, like an intricate maze. As they mature, they can rest in the knowledge that they will not be facing a similar fate as Dungeness Crabs, frequently seen on our dinner plates; Red Crabs have a shell that is just too thick.

RANGE: Southern California to Alaska

ZONE: low-tide line; subtidal to 300 ft

HABITATS: bays; eelgrass beds; rocky shores; tidepools

LENGTH: carapace to 4.25 in

WIDTH: carapace to 6.25 in

COLOR: deep reds

SIMILAR SPECIES: Dungeness Crab (p. 146)

Dungeness Crab

CANCER MAGISTER

I n spring you might be surprised to find countless crab shells on sandy beaches. These gray-brown, fan-shaped carapaces are not dead crabs, but the discards of the living. Look for ten sharp 'teeth' along the edge of the carapace, the tenth marking the widest point. Each crab will molt up to 15 times in its life. Molting is the precursor to the prolonged embrace of a male and female and the production of copious quantities of eggs.

OTHER NAME: Pacific Edible Crab

RANGE: Central and Northern California

ZONE: lower intertidal; subtidal to 755 ft

HABITATS: estuaries; bays; eelgrass beds; sandy tidepools

LENGTH: carapace to 6.4 in

WIDTH: carapace to 9.25 in

COLOR: gray-brown, purple tint

SIMILAR SPECIES: Red Crab (p. 145)

The Dungeness Crab prefers sandy offshore waters, but younger crabs can be found in the intertidal zone, lurking in Eelgrass (p. 201) or in the bottom of sandy tidepools. By day, the crabs bury themselves with only their eyes protruding above the sand. This crab prefers to chip away at clams with its stout, pale pincers, while it, in turn, is cracked open by people. A popular commercial catch, the Dungeness Crab is offered protection from exploitation— only male crabs that grow 6.5 inches or larger can be taken. Males have a narrower abdominal flap than the female, rather like a curled-under tail.

Purple Shore Crab

HEMIGRAPSUS NUDUS

The Purple Shore Crab is a feisty and aggressive little resident of the high and middle reaches of the intertidal zone. Often hiding under rocks by day, this crab can be identified by its deep purple color (but it also comes reddish-brown or green), and it is distinctive for the purple dots on its pincers. Three small 'teeth' define the edge of the carapace behind the eyes.

In Northern and Central California, the Purple Shore Crab can commonly be found from the wave-swept rocky shores to the calm waters of estuaries. Mussel beds, crevices and underneath rocks are the nooks where it will hide by day. By night at low tide, they emerge to scavenge and feed on bits of algae, sometimes venturing onto sandy beaches. Despite their herbivorous habits, they are defensive and will happily nip at you. In the quiet waters of estuaries and sounds, this crab will often share space with the Yellow Shore Crab (*H. oregonensis*). This paler and hairier version of the Purple Shore Crab prefers muddy areas.

RANGE: Southern California to Alaska

ZONE: intertidal

HABITATS: rocky shores; estuaries; under rocks

LENGTH: carapace to 2 in

WIDTH: carapace to 2.25 in

COLOR: variable purple, reddish-brown, olive-green

SIMILAR SPECIES: Black-clawed Mud Crab (p. 150), Striped Shore Crab (p. 148)

Striped Shore Crab

PACHYGRAPSUS CRASSIPES

The upper reaches of the intertidal zone are a favorite haunt for the charismatic Striped Shore Crab. This crab is versatile and adaptable, and you might come across it anywhere from rocky shores to the salty tidal creeks in estuaries. Where rocks lie on sand, gently turn them over to see if you can find this crab. In tidal creeks, look for their burrows along the soft, sandy banks. This shore crab is variably colored, sometimes reddish, other times black, but usually has green stripes running across the carapace. One spine is located behind each eye on the squarish carapace.

RANGE: Southern California to Oregon

ZONE: upper to middle intertidal

HABITATS: rocky shores; bays; mussel beds; estuaries; tidal creeks; pilings

LENGTH: carapace to 2 in

WIDTH: carapace to 2.5 in

COLOR: red, brown, black, green, green stripes

SIMILAR SPECIES: Purple Shore Crab (p. 147)

The Striped Shore Crab is very much a scavenger, feasting on pieces of seaweed, but it is occasionally more predatory, dining on limpets. Sometimes they can be observed rapidly scooping up tiny algae with their huge, spotted and striped claws. Get too close, and the crab will boldly present itself, claws outstretched, to encroaching beachcombers, and when it realizes just how big you are it will scurry away. Although a very happy crab on land, it occasionally returns to water to freshen up.

Green Crab
CARCINUS MAENAS

The Green Crab, a native resident of Europe, made a successful bid to colonize the Atlantic Coast, where it has become one of the commonest crabs. Now it has turned up in California. The Green Crab first made an appearance here in 1991, and is steadily marching up the coast. There is concern that it might alter the delicate ecological balance in California because it is such an aggressive predator with a huge appetite.

RANGE: Central and Northern California

ZONE: intertidal; subtidal to 20 ft

HABITATS: open coast; estuaries

LENGTH: carapace to 2.5 in

WIDTH: carapace to 3 in

COLOR: mottled, green and orange

The Green Crab is a mottled greenish or orange color. The legs and some of the underside can be mottled with reds. The carapace has five strong teeth down each side behind the eye, and the claws are long and strong. These claws are used to break open other crabs and clams. Watch out for this crab in estuaries and bays, where it likes the calmer waters. It is now widespread in the San Francisco Bay area, where it was first discovered, and is found further north. Only time will tell whether this alien species will become the common crab of the California coastline.

Black-clawed Mud Crab

LOPHOPANOPEUS BELLUS

Where gravel and sand combine, turn over larger rocks to reveal the Black-clawed Mud Crab: this pebble-sized crab thinks it is much larger, and will raise its black-tipped claws to ward off any naturalists that get too close. If you decide to ignore this aggressive posture, pick the crab up and it will play dead. Colors of this crab are very variable, coming in plain and mottled hues of brown, red or purple among others. The purple version might well be confused with the Purple Shore Crab, so be sure to look at its other features. The black-tipped pincers are a dead give-away.

The fan-shaped carapace has three prominent 'teeth' at the front corners. The chunky pincers pick apart all kinds of matter—this crab scavenges for bits and pieces of both plants and animals. Tucked away near the low-tide line, these crabs show up on rocky shores and in estuaries and bays, especially in tidepools and under algal holdfasts. Unlike most crabs, the female can mate when she has a hard shell—others have to molt.

OTHER NAME: Black-clawed Pebble Crab

RANGE: Central and Northern California

ZONE: lower intertidal; subtidal to 240 ft

HABITATS: estuaries; bays; rocks; cobbles; tidepools; algal holdfasts

LENGTH: carapace to 1 in

WIDTH: carapace to 1.4 in

COLOR: very variable, brown, red, purple, green

SIMILAR SPECIES: Purple Shore Crab (p. 147), Flat Porcelain Crab (p. 151)

Flat Porcelain Crab

PETROLISTHES CINCTIPES

When you turn rocks on beaches, the tiny crabs that scuttle away are likely to be Flat Porcelain Crabs. The rounded carapace is barely 1 inch in length, and the crabs are usually quite drab in their various shades of brown (and occasionally blue). The long antennae are a deep red, and the claws seem enormous compared to the size of the body. In counting the legs you will discover it has only four pairs, while most 'true' crabs have five pairs. Porcelain Crabs are filter feeders, sifting through the water for tiny particles of food.

RANGE: Southern California to British Columbia
ZONE: upper to middle intertidal
HABITATS: under rocks; stones; mussel beds
LENGTH: carapace to 1 in
COLOR: browns

This crab is very flat, which is an advantage when trying to squeeze into crevices or nooks on rocks or beds of California Mussel (p. 100). If its limb is caught, it will happily autotomize, or shed, that leg in order to escape. The lost leg soon regrows, so it is not a major loss to the crab. Its 'porcelain' name came from its apparent brittleness. Another huge-clawed but tiny crab is the Lumpy Porcelain Crab (*Pachycheles rudis*).

Shield-backed Kelp Crab
PUGETTIA PRODUCTA

This elegant crab has an attitude, so if you are tempted to pick one up, be warned, because the long legs and claws can reach much further than the average crab. The smooth but sharply spined carapace comes in various shades to match the seaweed on which the crab lives and dines—olive-green to reddish-brown shades are flecked with darker spots. Long limbs help these crabs grasp onto swaying kelp fronds. Watch for them grasping fronds of seaweed that wash back and forth in the surf. Sometimes an orange-brown crab will turn up in emerald Surf Grass (p. 200), in striking contrast.

RANGE: Southern California to Alaska

ZONE: lower intertidal; subtidal to 240 ft

HABITATS: rocky shores; kelp beds; tidepools

LENGTH: carapace to 4.75 in

WIDTH: carapace to 3.75 in

COLOR: variable reddish, brown, olive-green

The younger Shield-backed Kelp Crabs are intertidal, hidden under rocks and in tidepools. As they age, they tend to move into deeper water and kelp beds. In summer they will dine on kelp, but in winter, when much of the kelp has died, they become carnivores, extending their diet to barnacles and other intertidal organisms. The Sharp-nosed Crab (*Scyra acutifrons*) is smaller and tends to stick seaweed onto its spiky nose to help it blend in.

152

Turtle Crab

CRYPTOLITHODES SITCHENSIS

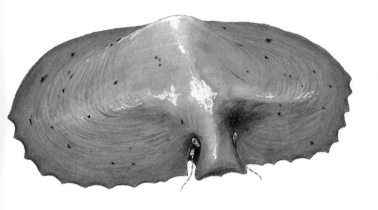

This odd crab is often overlooked because it resembles an empty clam or a lumpy sponge. The carapace is greatly extended so that all the legs and claws are tucked underneath and out of sight. The fringe of the carapace has a number of small teeth along the front and side edges. Two deep notches in the front mark the location of the eyes, and a prominent beak sticks out from between them. All these strange body formations are the crab's attempts to become invisible. To further the illusion, it moves only very slowly, so as not to draw attention to itself, feeding on small organisms from under its carapace as it goes. The color is very variable, sometimes mottled, sometimes plain, and can be red, brown, olive or sometimes white.

OTHER NAME: Umbrella Crab

RANGE: Southern California to Alaska

ZONE: lower intertidal; subtidal to 50 ft

HABITATS: rocks; rocky shores; quiet waters on or near open coast

LENGTH: to 2 in

WIDTH: carapace to 3 in

COLOR: variable, red, brown, gray, olive, white, mottled

Watch out for the Turtle Crab by rocks near the low-tide line. Quieter waters are preferred, in bays and by the open coast. It occurs along most of the coast of California where conditions are right. Remember that the odd stone or shell you just looked at might be a Turtle Crab.

Blue-handed Hermit Crab

PAGURUS SAMUELIS

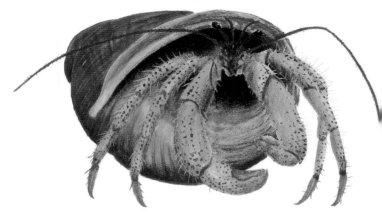

With their unusual preference for living in snail shells and their shy habit of hiding away, hermit crabs are one of the most popular intertidal animals. One of the commonest hermit crabs to be found is the Blue-handed Hermit Crab, the adult of which shows a distinct preference for the shells of the Black Tegula (p. 76). This hermit is olive to yellowish-green in color, and most distinct are the bright blue bands that are around the base of the legs. Its antennae are bright red.

OTHER NAME: Blueband Hermit

RANGE: Southern California to Alaska

ZONE: upper to lower intertidal; subtidal to 50 ft

HABITATS: open, rocky shores; tidepools

LENGTH: to 0.75 in

COLOR: olive-green to yellowish; blue bands

The carapace is striped and ends as a beak-like projection between the eyes. This projection and the bright blue band distinguish this hermit from the Grainy Hermit Crab (*P. granosimanus*), which is found lower in the intertidal zone. Hermit crabs have soft abdomens that they need to tuck away inside shells for protection. At the end of the abdomen is a hook-like tail that clings to the inside of the shell. As hermit crabs grow, they need to move into a larger shell. House moving must be done quickly—the crabs are very vulnerable to attack at moving time.

Acorn Barnacle
BALANUS GLANDULA

By far one of the most abundant animals to be found on rocky shores, these inconspicuous barnacles are easy to step over and ignore. Bend down a moment and study them! The Acorn Barnacle prefers the middle to upper intertidal zone where it is out of reach of predatory *Nucella* snails. So resilient are barnacles that an occasional ocean spray keeps them alive. During scorching sun or heavy rain, these tiny crustaceans, which are related to crabs and shrimps, close up their impenetrable plates like doors.

OTHER NAME: Common Barnacle

RANGE: Southern California to Alaska

ZONE: upper to middle intertidal

HABITATS: rocky shores

DIAMETER: to 0.6 in

COLOR: gray-white

Various small acorn barnacles (*Chthamalus* spp.) are only 0.1 inch across and are often seen growing next to the larger and paler Acorn Barnacle. The protective plates inside the 'crater' help identify which species you are looking at: the Small Acorn Barnacle has a religious cross, while the Acorn Barnacle has wavy edges. As the tide recedes, be sure to look into small tidepools filled with barnacles, and watch for their frantically waving 'cirri'—hand-like projections—that grasp for any tiny food particles left by the receding waters.

Giant Acorn Barnacle

BALANUS NUBILIS

Near the low-tide line of open coasts, it is possible to see this massive barnacle adhered to rocks, pilings or other hard surfaces. The Giant Acorn Barnacle is so large that the native peoples of the Northwest once ate it roasted. Sometimes the barnacles grow in bunches, on top of one another, until the mass becomes so thick and unstable that a storm can break it off at the base. Each barnacle is made from rough outer plates that are frequently encrusted with many different organisms. The inner plates are pointed and protect the cirri (hand-like projections) that come out to catch particles of food when the tide is in.

RANGE: Southern California to Alaska

ZONE: lower intertidal; subtidal to 300 ft

HABITATS: rocky shores; exposed coasts

DIAMETER: to 4 in

COLOR: gray-white plates; pinkish flesh

A barnacle is much like a shrimp that has landed on its head and built a wall around itself. This barnacle is almost as high as it is wide, and when the animal dies, the cavity left behind makes an ideal home for many organisms. Crabs such as the Oregon Cancer Crab (*Cancer oregonensis*) will hide away inside. An even larger barnacle is the Eagle Barnacle (*B. aquila*), growing to 5 inches or more.

Volcano Barnacle

TETRACLITA RUBESCENS

One of the most attractive barnacles to be found in California, from Sonoma County southwards, is the Volcano Barnacle. Looking very much like an idealized volcano, this sizable barnacle is found in the intertidal zone, from upper to lower levels, on rocky shores of the exposed coast. It is distinctive with its reddish hues, and ribs run down the sides of the barnacle, much like the lava streams on a volcano.

RANGE: Central and Southern California

ZONE: upper to lower intertidal

HABITATS: rocky, exposed shores; surge channels; overhangs

HEIGHT: to 2 in

DIAMETER: to 2 in

COLOR: reddish

Look in the surge channels and under overhangs for the Volcano Barnacle. It prefers the shadowed, darker corners of the intertidal world. A very similar barnacle is the Thatched Barnacle (*Semibalanus cariosus*); this barnacle also grows to an impressive two inches across its base, and can be found nearer the low-tide line. It shares the distinctive ribs, but lacks the reddish hues found in the Volcano Barnacle. The Thatched Barnacle also has a more northerly range and can be found all the way up into the Pacific Northwest. Faded Volcano Barnacles might be confused with the Thatched Barnacle, so look for a proportionally smaller opening in the Volcano Barnacle.

Common Goose Barnacle

LEPAS ANATIFERA

After a violent storm, be sure to hike the sandy beaches for articles that have drifted in from the high seas. Aside from disheartening garbage, there is often driftwood sculpted by years in the ocean. Inside the wood are many Pacific Shipworms (p. 86), and outside are the strange Common Goose Barnacles. These creatures can be found in large colonies on anything that has been floating in the sea, including plastic and styrofoam. The tiny nauplius (barnacle larva) swims in open waters until attracted to the shade of something floating—here it sticks for good.

OTHER NAME: Pelagic Goose Barnacle

RANGE: Central California to Alaska

ZONE: offshore; pelagic; open ocean

HABITATS: on floats stranded on beaches

LENGTH: to 6 in

COLOR: black stalk; white shell

SIMILAR SPECIES: Leaf Barnacle (p. 159)

Common Goose Barnacles might not look like the barnacles stuck on rock, but they are closely related. A thick, fleshy stalk supports the crustacean. Smooth, white plates form a shell surrounding the rest of the animal's body, and when submerged, the cirri (hand-like projections) are extended out to filter the water with fine hairs. Each plate is bordered in yellow. When these barnacles drift onto the shore, baking sunshine soon kills them, and gasping barnacles can be seen hanging out of their home.

Leaf Barnacle
POLLICIPES POLYMERUS

Leaf Barnacles are frequently found on the exposed coast in thick clusters stuck amidst beds of California Mussel (p. 100). These peculiar bunches of crustaceans thrive in the pounding surf—surge channels and very exposed rocks being the favored locations. They differ from the Common Goose Barnacle in that they stick to rocks on shore, and have many smaller plates protecting the animal inside. The stalk is a deep reddish-black and covered in minuscule spines that are arranged in neat rows. These stalks are tough and rubbery to cope with the stress of stormy seas.

OTHER NAME: Goose Barnacle

RANGE: Southern California to Alaska

ZONE: upper to lower intertidal

HABITATS: rocky shores; mussel beds

LENGTH: to 3.25 in

COLOR: dark stalk; whitish plates

SIMILAR SPECIES: Common Goose Barnacle (p. 158)

As waves break over the rocks, the barnacles open and stretch out their cirri to catch the backwash off the rocks. Their hope is to rake in any small organisms washed off their footings. When closed, dark red 'lips' mark where the cirri come out. If you pass your hand over the top so that your shadow passes over them, notice how they twist and retract a little bit. Why they do so is a mystery, but obviously they are light sensitive.

Smooth Skeleton Shrimp

CAPRELLA LAEVIUSCULA

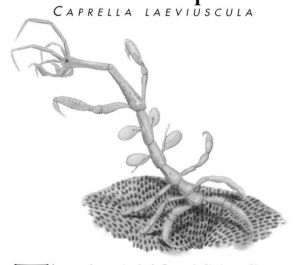

The peculiar and rakish Smooth Skeleton Shrimp clings to hydroids, algae and Eelgrass (p. 201) in both rocky and sandy shores. The last three pairs of the shrimp's legs have hooks for feet, and these hooks help the creature grasp tightly and securely to its perch. From here it waves gently back and forth, consuming tiny animals suspended in the water, pieces of algae and single-celled plants.

RANGE: Southern California to British Columbia

ZONE: lower intertidal; shallow subtidal

HABITATS: eelgrass beds; algae; hydroids; rocky and sandy areas

LENGTH: to 2 in

COLOR: variable green, tan, pinkish

Although it carries the name 'shrimp,' it is not a true shrimp, but belongs to a group of crustaceans called 'amphipods.' The highly jointed body bears numerous appendages and claws, and it comes in shades of green, tan or pinkish, depending on which color is the most suitable for camouflage. Occasionally, skeleton shrimps, of which there are a number of different species, can be seen clinging in clusters together with their arms outstretched. Like strange beasts from another planet, these animals deserve some close inspection with a hand lens so that you can see their strange body shape and curious behavior.

Barred Shrimp
HEPTACARPUS PUGETTENSIS

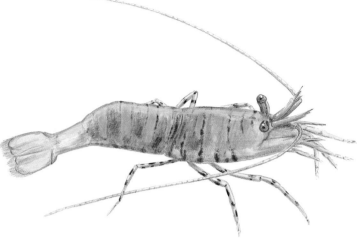

What looks like a still tidepool one moment can become a surprising mass of shrimp the next. Many different kinds of *Heptacarpus* shrimps are found along the coast of California, all of which are distinguished by the kink in their back, giving them the collective common name of 'Broken Back Shrimps.' They are often quite motionless during the bright daylight hours, and because of their excellent camouflage you can be forgiven for not noticing them. Broken Back Shrimps come in all colors, and many are partially translucent, allowing them to blend in further. Poke around awhile and you might notice them when they scurry off at great speed.

OTHER NAME: Broken Back Shrimp

RANGE: Central California to British Columbia

ZONE: low-tide line; subtidal to 50 ft

HABITATS: rocky shores; under rocks; tidepools

LENGTH: to 1 in

COLOR: tan, yellow, red stripes

The Barred Shrimp is just one example of the Broken Back Shrimps. They have yellowish bands across the abdomen, and red and yellow stripes here and there on the body. The delicate legs have reddish bands around them, too. Look around the bottom edge of boulders and under rocks for gatherings of these small shrimp. Sometimes Barred Shrimps will gather in large numbers. They are scavengers, feeding on anything that takes their fancy.

Vosnesensky's Isopod

I D O T E A   W O S N E S E N S K I I

An isopod is a type of crustacean and Vosnesensky was a Russian zoologist who collected these appealing creatures in the nineteenth century—together they give this species a name that seems more appropriate for a small spaceship. These creatures are most often green, but will assume many colors to help them blend in with the background. Most stunning are the isopods, in various shades of mottled pink, found on encrusting algae. Black, red and brown versions also occur.

OTHER NAME: Rockweed Isopod

RANGE: Southern California to Alaska

ZONE: upper to lower intertidal; subtidal to 53 ft

HABITATS: exposed and quiet rocky shores; mussel beds; seaweed; tidepools

LENGTH: to 1.4 in

COLOR: highly variable, green, pink, brown, red, black

Tucked away under rocks by day, they venture out at night and can be seen swimming across tidepools. Where there are accumulations of rotting seaweed, a higher chance exists of encountering the flattened isopod and its seven pairs of legs. Mussel beds provide plenty of cover for them, too. Similar but gray and smaller is Harford's Greedy Isopod (*Cirolana harfordi*), which can be found in a number of places, such as under rocks and in mussel beds where it feeds on any bits and pieces of dead animals. If you come across something dead, you are sure to come across this greedy character getting its fill.

Western Sea Roach

LIGIA OCCIDENTALIS

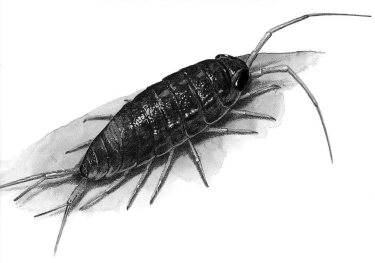

Near and above the high-tide line, this cockroach-like creature stays tucked out of sight during the day. As the light fades, however, the Western Sea Roach crawls out from hiding in the cracks and crevices and starts to feed on the thin film of algae covering the rocks. By day, turn over a rock and you might well scare one or two of these roaches. They will run for cover in another sheltered spot. Although these crustaceans prefer life at the limits of high tide, they are still dependent on the moisture of the sea; sometimes they can be seen crawling down to the edge of the tidepool where they dip their rear end into the water to moisten up the soft gills inside.

RANGE: Southern California to Alaska
ZONE: high-tide line and above
HABITATS: under rocks; crevices
LENGTH: to 1 in
COLOR: brown, tan, gray

The Western Sea Roach can be found south from Sonoma County. Overlapping part of its range and abundant in Northern California, is the similar Rock Louse (*L. pallasi*). This louse grows longer and often wider. Compare the lengths of the rear appendages—if they are very short, then it is a Rock Louse.

California Beach Flea

MEGALORCHESTIA CALIFORNIANA

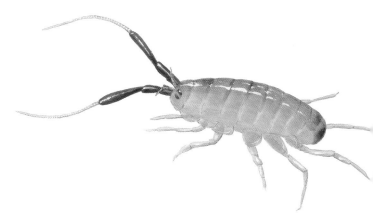

Amidst the wrack cast up on beaches at the high-tide line, thousands of small jumping creatures are tucked away. On exposed, sandy beaches most of these creatures are California Beach Fleas. By day they rest and keep moist, either in their burrows or under mats of kelp decomposing on the shore. By night, they come out in the thousands to feast on the latest kelp delivery from the sea. The beach fleas follow the waves down the beach, and retreat before the tide comes in.

OTHER NAME: *Orchestoidea californiana*

RANGE: Southern California to British Columbia

ZONE: high-tide line and above

HABITATS: sandy beaches

LENGTH: to 1.1 in

COLOR: tan; red antennae

With a sandy-colored body and bright red antennae, these are attractive crustaceans. Younger individuals have darker patches down their back. Unfortunately, many people are put off by the sheer number of fleas and their writhing jumping madness when disturbed. That they are called fleas doesn't help their reputation at all, because California Beach Fleas do not bite. Strong back legs give them an enormous athletic talent for jumping, earning them their common name. A smaller and drabber version is the Beach Hopper (*Traskorchestia traskiana*) of bays and quieter beaches.

Tapered Flatworm

NOTOPLANA ACTICOLA

When looking under the rocks of the intertidal zone, you are likely overlooking the common Tapered Flatworm, because it resembles more of a thin film of goo than a living animal. Sometimes it is so flat that it appears to be translucent. Usually the color of the Tapered Flatworm is tan or gray, sometimes mottled, with some noticeable eyespots nearer the broader front end. Flatworms also have eyespots around the edge of the body, but these are often too small to be seen with the naked eye. Being so flat they are quite capable of crawling into minute crevices. By day flatworms will remain under rocks, but they will emerge and glide about at night.

RANGE: California
ZONE: upper to lower intertidal
HABITATS: under and on rocks; crevices
LENGTH: to 2.5 in
COLOR: tan, gray

Flatworms are an unusual group of worms. They have a big mouth on the underside, and with this mouth they tend to gulp down their prey. Tapered Flatworms will dine on small invertebrates, even limpets half their size. They can glide rapidly about using tiny hairs on their underside. A simple gut spreads down the middle of the worm, and the mouth must be used to excrete waste as well.

Variable Nemertean

TUBULANUS POLYMORPHUS

This nemertean, or ribbon worm, is an unusual find among mussel beds, algal growths or other well-covered, rocky surfaces in which it can crawl about. Its soft orange, red or yellow body lacks any distinctive markings. These worms can be enormously long, stretching out to a staggering 9 feet, yet will only be a few inches when contracted. Despite this elasticity, the Variable Nemertean is very fragile, so please do not tug at it because it could fall apart in your hands!

Like all nemerteans, it is a carnivore, and it has the disturbing habit of reversing its proboscis out of its head to catch its prey. By squeezing a few muscles here and there, the pressure forces the sticky mouthpart out onto the prey. Armed with small arrows and venom, the prey is caught by the proboscis, and then usually swallowed whole. Another giant, stretchy ribbon worm is the Six-lined Nemertean (*T. sexlineatus*), which is chocolate-brown and wrapped in lines of white, around and down its length. This one doesn't stretch to such great lengths, reaching its limit at about 3 feet.

OTHER NAME: Orange Nemertean

RANGE: Central California to Alaska

ZONE: intertidal

HABITATS: rocky shores; mussel beds

LENGTH: to 9 ft

COLOR: yellow, orange, red

Fifteen-scaled Worm

HARMATHOE IMBRICATA

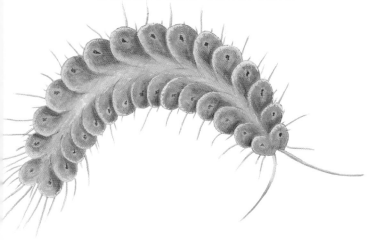

This strange armored creature inhabits many corners of the intertidal zone, tucked away under algal holdfasts or under tidepool rocks. It is very hardy, enjoying all kinds of conditions from the low-salinity waters of estuaries to the bitterly cold and dark depths of 11,000 feet. This worm, with 15 pairs of scales running down each side, also turns up in the tubes of other worms and the shells of hermit crabs. Its color varies enormously from red to black to green, with additional markings of dots or stripes. Commonest is the gray-green form.

The scales down the back serve as a brooding chamber for the eggs, which are very easily dislodged, so be careful if you are inclined to handle such creatures. These worms are carnivores and rather intolerant of their own kind—if confined in the same container, some scale worms will readily bite each other. Very similar and found in the same habitats is the Twelve-scaled Worm (*Lepidonotus squamatus*), which grows to the same size as the Fifteen-scaled Worm. Much larger at over 4 inches is the Eighteen-scaled Worm (*Halosydna brevitosa*).

RANGE: Southern California to Alaska

ZONE: lower intertidal; subtidal to 11,000 ft

HABITATS: tidepools; under rocks; holdfasts; estuaries; open shores; mussel beds

LENGTH: to 2.5 in

COLOR: gray-green, highly variable to red, yellow, black

Clam Worm

NEREIS VEXILLOSA

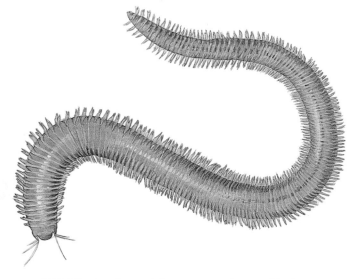

This bristly annelid worm occurs in mussel beds on the open coast and under rocks and driftwood in bays. During summer nights in quiet bays, these worms will often swarm and wriggle about in great numbers at the surface of the water to breed. An individual is more often encountered creeping its way about, looking for chunks of seaweed or animals to bite off with its strange mouth. The complex mouthpart comes right out of the worm's head, so that it can bite more successfully. If you find one, gently squeeze it behind the head and the mouthpart will emerge.

OTHER NAME: Mussel Worm

RANGE: California to Alaska

ZONE: intertidal

HABITATS: rocks; mussel beds; wood; quiet bays; open coast

LENGTH: to 6 in

COLOR: gray, with iridescence

This worm is segmented, and the bristly appendages on each segment help the worm move about. The base color is mostly grayish, with an iridescence that gives the worm hues of green, pink or blue. This Clam Worm grows to about 6 inches in length. A smaller, similar *N. grubei* grows to 4 inches. A close relative, the Lug Worm (*Abarenicola pacifica*) has taken to burying itself in mud of quiet bays—evidence for which can be seen from the muddy casts left at low tide.

Red Tube Worm

SERPULA VERMICULARIS

When you turn rocks at low tide, you might overlook a dead-looking crusty tube. This calcareous tube, often covered with marine growth, is home to the Red Tube Worm, and is well worth further investigation. When immersed in water, a brilliant display of red gills is pushed out of the sinuous tube. There are 40 pairs of gills with which the worm feeds and breathes. The body of the worm is tucked safely away inside the tube. Some worms have pink gills; others are banded in white.

OTHER NAME:	Calcareous Tube Worm
RANGE:	Southern California to Alaska
ZONE:	lower intertidal; subtidal to 300 ft
HABITATS:	under rocks, shells, pilings
LENGTH:	to 4 in
COLOR:	white tube; red, pink or whitish gills

Any firm surface covered with water makes a good home, and the distinctive tubes turn up on pilings and shells. When the feeding worm is disturbed, the gills are withdrawn in a flash and the entrance to the tube is sealed off with a red, funnel-shaped operculum. Empty tubes are obvious because they lack this bright red door. Similar but minuscule by comparison is the Tiny Tube Worm (*Spirorbis borealis*), which is commonly found on hard surfaces immersed in water and grows to a mere eighth of an inch.

Curly Terebellid Worm

THELEPUS CRISPUS

A number of worms have the habit of burying their soft and vulnerable bodies in the sand and gravel, and coating themselves in a wall of mucus and grit. Most common is the Curly Terebellid Worm found on rocky and gravelly shores, sometimes under rocks or peeking out of crevices. The top part of the tube protrudes from the sand and is very tough. Grit and small stones stick to the mucus, which then hardens. The tube is tough enough to withstand the rough life on the open coast. Concealed inside is a long, reddish worm that grows to 6 inches in length and up to 11 inches exceptionally.

OTHER NAME: Spaghetti Worm

RANGE: Southern California to Alaska

ZONE: middle to lower intertidal; subtidal to 50 ft

HABITATS: rocky, gravelly shores; sand; open coast

LENGTH: to 11 in

COLOR: pinkish tentacles; reddish body

Out of the top of the tube emerge translucent, pinkish tentacles and some thin, reddish gills. The tentacles can reach 12 inches in length, and gently pick their way about the surface collecting tiny particles of food. When disturbed they are withdrawn quickly, but they can break off. In such an event, the tentacles continue to writhe around on their own, much as a beheaded chicken would.

Giant Feather Duster

EUDISTYLIA POLYMORPHA

It is hard to believe, but this beautiful crown of feathers is, in fact, part of a worm. Peer over the edge of a wharf in a clean harbor, and you are sure to see some of these Giant Feather Dusters attached to pilings or submerged wood. These creatures also hang from the sides of surge channels, and can be witnessed in their full glory in rocky tidepools. Some are deeply embedded in crevices, so that the long tube is almost invisible, while others grow in small groups and the long tubes can be very obvious. Inside this tube, the body of the worm is protected.

The feathery feeding apparatus is often red, but can be tan, orange, brown and sometimes banded. This apparatus filters small particles from the water, as well as absorbs oxygen to breathe. Giant Feather Dusters are sensitive creatures, and a gentle touch to their feathery appendages will result in a speedy withdrawal deep into their tube. The crown is about 3 inches in diameter, and emerges from a tube that can be as much as 11 inches long, but seldom is all of the tube seen.

RANGE: Southern California to Alaska

ZONE: lower intertidal; subtidal to 1400 ft

HABITATS: bays; harbors; pilings; open coast; surge channels; tidepools

LENGTH: tube to 11 in

DIAMETER: crown to 3 in

COLOR: tan, red, orange, brown; sometimes banded

SIMILAR SPECIES: Ostrich Plume Hydroid (p. 175)

Stearn's Sea Spider

PYCNOGONUM STEARNSI

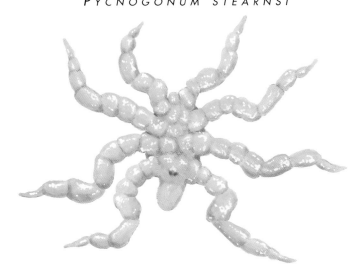

Small and peculiar, the Sea Spider, which is not a spider at all, looks fit for casting in a horror film. Eight legs give it the sinister flair associated with spiders, hence its name, but it is, in fact, a Pycnogonid. This small creature is all legs. Its abdomen is almost nonexistent, and most of the head is a stout proboscis that it inserts into its prey, and then it sucks out the victim's juices. Small but distinct eyes are set just behind the proboscis. Stearn's Sea Spider comes in gentle shades of yellow to pink.

RANGE: Central California to Alaska

ZONE: middle to lower intertidal

HABITATS: tidepools; rocks; anemones; tunicates

LENGTH: to 0.5 in

COLOR: yellow to pink

If you are determined to find a sea spider, a good source location is the base and column of the Giant Green Anemone (p. 139). Here, small gatherings can be observed feeding. Other anemones also fall prey to these suckers. The Clawed Sea Spider (*Phoxichilidium femoratum*) grows to only 0.1 inch in length, but has comparatively long legs. The Clawed Sea Spider is so small that you are sure to miss it. Sea spiders are a role model for modern times: the male looks after and carries the eggs until they hatch.

Kelp Encrusting Bryozoan

MEMBRANIPORA MEMBRANACEA

Storm-tossed kelp might not be the first place you would think to look for mysterious marine organisms, but be sure to pick through some Bull Kelp (p. 186) or Giant Perennial Kelp (p. 185) anyway. Closely hugging the surface of the algae, you might find distinctive pale, delicate mats—lacy filigrees of calcareous walls surrounding hundreds of tiny organisms. These are the Kelp Encrusting Bryozoans. Bryozoans come in so many shapes and sizes—some resembling mossy mats, others looking like branching corals.

Each white patch is a whole colony of animals that resemble miniature anemones, with their circular hand of food-catching tentacles. Tiny walls house and separate each individual bryozoan, and the colony expands from the middle outwards, often giving them a round formation. Close inspection in a tub of water with a hand lens is worthwhile, because the tiny creatures will emerge from their protective homes to feed. Look out for a small patch of jelly-like substance that matches the bryozoan colors perfectly—you might be looking at the 0.6-inch long Doridella Sea Slug (*Doridella steinbergae*), which browses exclusively on this bryozoan.

OTHER NAME: Lacy-crust Bryozoan

RANGE: Southern California to Alaska

ZONE: subtidal

HABITATS: kelp

LENGTH: colony variable to several inches

COLOR: white, cream, gray

Rosy Bryozoan

EURYSTOMELLA BILABIATA

There are many different kinds of animals and algae that creep, spread and grow on rocks to form carpets and encrustations. It is a challenge trying to determine just what one is, even for the most knowledgeable of scientists, so do not despair! One such organism that you might come across, and might be able to identify, is the Rosy Bryozoan. This encrustation is pinkish or red, often blotched with brown, and where the tiny organisms have died, the bryozoan can be covered with small, green algae.

RANGE: Southern California to Alaska

ZONE: middle to low intertidal

HABITATS: rocks

LENGTH: colony variable to several inches

COLOR: pink, red, brown

Rosy Bryozoan colonies start off very small, and gradually spread out from the central point, usually resulting in a roughly circular formation. This bryozoan develops with a typical pattern that is governed by the positioning of each individual organism in its walled home. This pattern is often described as a basket-weave. One of the most rewarding features of these pretty encrustations is not the bryozoan itself, but the potential to find the exquisite pink Hopkin's Rose (p. 114) that almost exclusively lives, feeds and breeds on this bryozoan.

Ostrich Plume Hydroid

AGLAOPHENIA LATIROSTRIS

While inspecting the walls and overhangs of surge channels on exposed rocky shores, you might find the feathery colonies of the Ostrich Plume Hydroid. Keep an eye open for the rising tide though, because surge channels are very dangerous places. These hydroids are cnidarians, and are closely related to the anemones, although they certainly don't look related. Each colony consists of a number of stems that have many branches. Examine these branches closely, with a hand lens, and on each branch you should be able to make out individual hydroids in a neat line. Rings of tentacles on each hydroid catch tiny organisms and particles on which the hydroids feed.

RANGE: Southern California to Alaska

ZONE: middle to low intertidal; subtidal

HABITATS: overhangs; surge channels; rocky shores

LENGTH: each 'feather' to 4 in

COLOR: variable, reddish

SIMILAR SPECIES: Giant Feather Duster (p. 171)

Spend some time poking around these feathery bunches because, with a bit of detective work you might stumble across one of the peculiar Smooth Skeleton Shrimps (p. 160). These shrimps dine on the hydroids, and are often well camouflaged amidst the tangle of hydroid branches. If you are nosing around in red Ostrich Plume Hydroids, then expect to find red shrimp. Don't confuse these feathery hydroids with the Giant Feather Duster, which is actually a worm.

Boring Sponge
CLIONA CELATA

With a somewhat misleading name, this yellow sponge actually has an interesting story to tell. Usually found growing on barnacles and shells, especially the Giant Rock Scallop (p. 85), and clams and oysters, the Boring Sponge is a small recycling depot. Special cells secrete sulfuric acid that eats away at the calcium carbonate, which makes up a shell. This process creates a honeycomb of channels, and the shell eventually disintegrates, which keeps the sea from clogging up with piles of abandoned shells. The sponge does not discriminate—dead shells are just as good as the living. The compounds that make up the shells are then recycled by the sponge back into the marine system and are once again available for use by other animals—perhaps even by another snail carefully crafting its mobile palace.

RANGE: Southern California to Alaska
ZONE: intertidal; subtidal to 400 ft
HABITATS: shells; barnacles
DIAMETER: to 12 in
COLOR: yellow

The sponge appears as small, yellow dots and pores on the shell surface, until it grows so large that it can completely smother the host. While beachcombing, be sure to study shell fragments for the small holes and honeycomb matrix that the sponge leaves behind.

176

Purple Sponge

HALICLONA PERMOLLIS

Soft, smooth and purple, these sponges don't appear to be animals, but they are, albeit primitive. The gorgeously colored Purple Sponge is found encrusting hard surfaces in calmer waters and tidepools. Close inspection will reveal tiny holes in the surface. The really small holes are incurrent holes, inside of which are small cells with beating flagella on them that draw in water. The large holes, which resemble volcanoes, are called 'oscula,' and it is from these that the water flows out.

Sponges are not the most dynamic of animals, their attractive colors being one of the few things that make them stand out. What they do is limited to pumping water through the extensive matrix, sifting the water for microscopic particles on which they dine. The matrix is supported by tiny spicules made of silica, or glass, and hungry sea slugs put these to use in their own skin. One such hungry sea slug is the Ring-spotted Doris (p. 110). The similar gray-green Crumb-of-bread Sponge (*Halichondria panicea*) has a texture resembling bread, and is found in the same range and further north.

RANGE: Central California to Alaska

ZONE: middle to lower intertidal; subtidal to 20 ft

HABITATS: hard surfaces; protected shores

DIAMETER: to 36 in

COLOR: pink to purple

Velvety Red Sponge

OPHLITASPONGIA PENNATA

Vibrant dashes of red splashed about on rocks are most likely the brilliant Velvety Red Sponge. This common sponge prefers the open coasts, but seeks out overhangs and darker crevices. Encrusting and very flat, it occurs from the middle intertidal zone down to subtidal waters. As its name implies, it is soft and velvety to the touch and tiny pores pockmark its entire surface.

RANGE: Southern California to British Columbia

ZONE: middle intertidal; shallow subtidal

HABITATS: rocks; dark crevices; open coasts

DIAMETER: to 36 in

COLOR: red

Get down on your hands and knees to observe the sponge closely, because like most large patches, it is guarding a little secret. As illustrated, you might be able to make out the tiny and adorable Crimson Doris (*Rostanga pulchra*). This sea slug matches the sponge's color to perfection, thus making it hard to notice. The little slug seldom wanders from the sponge that it feeds on and lays eggs on—if it did the slug would become obvious because of its dazzling color. The Crimson Doris barely grows to half an inch in length. Eggs, also bright red, are laid in little coils on the sponge.

Sea Pork

APLIDIUM CALIFORNICUM

For those with a bit of imagination, colonies of these encrusting animals might look like a slab of pork. Sea Pork is actually a low-growing mass of tunicates, or sea squirts. These organisms are filter feeders, with an intake and outlet for water to pass through, and they favor very clean water. Where wave action is strong, it is possible to see these creatures. Sea squirts come in various shapes and sizes, and the Sea Pork is a colonial form, of which there are many different species determined in part by their color. Sea Porks usually come in pinkish hues, but white and brown are common shades.

RANGE: Southern California to Alaska

ZONE: lower intertidal; subtidal to 1200 ft

HABITATS: wave-washed rocks; open coasts

DIAMETER: to 8 in

COLOR: variable, white, pink, brown

These colonies are smooth to the touch, and resemble some sponges, but there the similarity ends. Sea squirts are sophisticated equivalents of sponges, but are not related to them. Sea spiders can sometimes be found sticking their mouths in and feeding on the Sea Pork, and some snails favor the occasional meal. Food for the Sea Pork is the microscopic component of the water that it filters—bacteria and single-celled plants and animals.

Monterey Stalked Tunicate

STYELA MONTEREYENSIS

This tunicate is distinctive for its long stalk and tough body, with two valves, or siphons, at the top. It is a solitary tunicate, unlike the large colonies of Sea Pork (p. 179) or Lightbulb Tunicate (p.181), and it can often be found suspended from over-hangs in quieter corners of surge channels. The protected side of rocks on exposed coasts is favored, and pilings where the water is clean might harbor several individuals. The main body of the animal is wrinkled longitudinally, and the tex-ture is tough and almost woody. The color varies from yellowish to red-brown. Sometimes the tunicate is covered with other organisms, although this seldom happens when it is growing where there are swift currents.

OTHER NAME: Stalked Sea Squirt

RANGE: Southern California to British Columbia

ZONE: lower intertidal; subtidal to 100 ft

HABITATS: surge channels; rocks; open and protected coasts; pilings

LENGTH: to 10 in

COLOR: tan to red-brown

Surprisingly, we have quite a lot in common with sea squirts. A free-swimming larval tunicate has a primitive spinal cord, a stomach and a heart, and is not unlike a human when first developing. As they age, though, this resemblance fades and the cord disappears. As the larva grows, it decides to settle down on a rock, taking on its new adult form.

Lightbulb Tunicate

CLAVELINA HUNTSMANI

In the intertidal zone of Central California, you might be surprised to find a patch of organisms that bear a striking resemblance to lightbulbs—it is as if they have glowing filaments inside their transparent bodies. These filaments are part of the internal organs of tunicates and are white or pinkish. Sometimes the tunicates have small, bright orange embryos inside the 'bulb'—these are the young being brooded until they are large and old enough to leave the parent.

Spring and summer are the best times to find these tunicates because many die off during winter months. North of Monterey Bay it is hard to find them intertidally, because they have retreated into the subtidal waters. The shadier recesses of large rocks, overhangs and ledges are preferred, and here Lightbulb Tunicates can form colonies up to 20 inches across. These colonies are the result of one tunicate budding off another. Tunicates are frequently the victims of the predatory attentions of some snails and seas slugs—as they are firmly rooted to the spot, there is little chance of escape.

RANGE: Southern California to British Columbia

ZONE: lower intertidal; subtidal to 100 ft

HABITATS: shaded, rocky areas; ledges; overhangs; open coast

HEIGHT: to 2 in

DIAMETER: colony to 20 in

COLOR: translucent body; pink or white 'filament'

Winged Kelp
ALARIA MARGINATA

Winged kelp is one of the larger brown algae of the Pacific Coast and comes in variable shades of olive-green to dark brown. The long, smooth blade has a wavy edge and a strong midrib that has formed from the stipe, or stalk, at the base. So long is the blade that in rough seas the end is whipped about, giving it a tattered appearance. Just above the small but tenacious holdfast is a cluster of smaller blades that are specialized to produce spores. These spores will eventually become whole new kelps. Winged Kelp is one of the larger and more distinct species of *Alaria* kelps, of which there are several species to be found.

This kelp makes excellent and nutritious dining, especially for stir-fries and soups or as a wrap for other foods. If biting down on rubbery kelp appeals to you, when harvesting be sure to leave the base of the kelp with its cluster of small reproductive blades. Leaving it alone will allow the kelp to produce many more individuals, and ensure a healthy sustainable harvest.

RANGE: Central California to Alaska
ZONE: low intertidal; shallow subtidal
HABITATS: rocky shores
LENGTH: to 10 ft
WIDTH: to 8 in
COLOR: olive green, dark brown
SIMILAR SPECIES: Oar Weed Kelp (p. 184)

Feather Boa
EGREGIA MENZIESII

This exotic-looking brown alga is a common kelp of the exposed and semi-protected coasts from Southern California northwards. One of the largest intertidal brown algae, it grows to impressive lengths. It is noticeable for its many small blades (to 2 inches in length) growing off the side of the main stem, or stipe. Some of these blades are enlarged into bulbous floats. The illustration shows just one small portion of a long blade. The upper section of the main blade is a golden-brown, while other parts can be olive-green to dark brown.

The Shield-backed Kelp Crab (p. 152) often makes its home here, and takes on brown coloration to match the kelp. In addition, a small limpet, less than 1 inch in length, lives on the stipe and is found nowhere else. This limpet (*Lottia insessa*) is brown and leaves small depressions in the main stem. Feather Boa is common in California, but starts to become increasingly scarce from Oregon northwards. On farms this kelp has often been used as rich mulch, rivaling manure.

RANGE: British Columbia to California

ZONE: lower intertidal; shallow subtidal

HABITATS: rocky shores

LENGTH: to 15 ft

WIDTH: to 6 in

COLOR: olive-green to dark brown

Oar Weed Kelp
LAMINARIA ANDERSONII

When the tide is at its lowest, groves of Oar Weed Kelp can be seen poking through the water, looking abandoned by the sea. The strong stipes, to 2 feet in length, stick up while supporting a tattered, drooping blade. When the strong waves of the rocky coasts return, they give the standing kelp bed a strong thrashing, allowing the rubbery qualities of the kelp to demonstrate their toughness. The Oar Weed Kelp grows in surge channels where the surf comes pounding in. In such rough conditions, the blade of the kelp splits many times, which gives it a tattered appearance. Come the year's end, these blades are lost, but the stipe remains and will soon produce another blade.

OTHER NAME: Split Whip Wrack

RANGE: Central California to Washington

ZONE: lower intertidal; shallow subtidal

HABITATS: exposed, rocky shores; surge channels

LENGTH: to 5 ft

WIDTH: blade to 18 in

COLOR: dark brown, olive-green

SIMILAR SPECIES: Winged Kelp (p. 182), Sea Palm (p. 187)

Blades of this brown alga can be as wide as 18 inches, and the whole kelp might reach lengths of 5 feet. There are several similar kelps in the genus of *Laminaria*. Another kelp that has a broad, tattered blade is the short-stiped Winged Kelp, and the Sea Palm has a similar drooping habit.

Giant Perennial Kelp

MACROCYSTIS SPP.

Giant forests of kelp lie just off-shore on the open coast where the surf is not too strong. A huge ball of a holdfast ties their great length (to 40 feet) down to the seafloor. The stem branches many times, each ending with a series of slim blades. The uppermost section of a kelp frond is illustrated (above), and shows the tapered blades with their bulbous bases. These bulbs are gas-filled, which keeps the kelp near the water surface. The grooved blades, to 2 feet in length, are a deep greenish-brown, with toothed edges. New leaf-like blades form by the topmost blade, splitting in half repeatedly.

RANGE: Southern California to Alaska

ZONE: low-tide line; subtidal to 33 ft

HABITATS: rocky shores

LENGTH: to 40 ft

COLOR: dark greenish-brown

The kelp forest's immense productivity is harvested off some coasts—but only the top 3 feet are taken, allowing the kelp to continue growing. This kelp produces 'algin,' a substance with many uses, such as giving ice cream the texture we all love. Storms also take their usual cut of weaker kelp, casting them up in huge piles of wrack. Refer to the Sea Otter (p. 32) for a story about the past demise of these great forests.

Bull Kelp
NEREOCYSTIS LUETKEANA

A common brown alga of the West Coast, the Bull Kelp is also one of the most popular. It has some impressive statistics, growing up to 80 feet long, and is secured by a massive holdfast that is as much as 16 inches across. Most incredibly is that this growth occurs in one summer season. By early winter the kelp are dying, and storms toss their distinctive form up on shores where beachcombers are enthralled by them.

A very obvious feature is the large, bulbous float that is up to 4.5 inches in diameter. This thick-walled vessel is filled with gas and keeps the lengthy fronds afloat. At low tide, they can be seen just offshore, bobbing in the gentle waves. The tough, hollow stipes take months to rot, and have been used as fishing line. The dark greenish-brown blades grow off two nodes on the float, and reach the length of 10 feet. Stranded stipes, when sliced and pickled, are excellent to eat.

OTHER NAME: Bull Whip
RANGE: Southern California to Alaska
ZONE: shallow subtidal
HABITATS: exposed, rocky shores
LENGTH: to 80 ft
COLOR: dark greenish-brown

Sea Palm
POSTELSIA PALMAEFORMIS

On the most exposed rocks where the surf smashes in full force, the Sea Palm can be seen growing in tree-like groves. A thick, rubbery stem bends with the force of the waves, springing back up once each wave subsides. From the top of the hollow stem, numerous flattened blades hang down. A young Sea Palm is green, but as it ages it takes on the brownish hues typical of the brown algae family. This plant is annual, living only one summer season and growing from fresh seeds every year.

Its exposed location requires a tough holdfast that sends root-like extensions into the rocky crevices. California Mussel (p. 100) and Acorn Barnacle (p. 155) beds are frequently interspersed with clusters of this beautiful kelp. The Sea Palm makes an excellent addition to stir-fries, and is just as good eaten fresh. But its location is a hazardous one, so be sure to keep an eye on the surf if you are tempted to grab a handful. In addition, don't take too much—you will jeopardize the ability of that grove to regenerate next year.

RANGE: Central California to Alaska
ZONE: upper to middle intertidal
HABITATS: exposed, rocky shores
HEIGHT: to 20 in
COLOR: green to olive-brown

Rockweed

FUCUS DISTICHUS

Anyone clambering about the rocks when the tide is out will have come across the successful Rockweeds. There are several similar species, and they typically grow on rocks in the middle intertidal zone. Thick, drooping clumps hang down from the tops of rocks in shades of olive-green to yellowish-green; they are almost black when they dry out. This alga is a member of the brown algae family, despite having greenish tones! A shoot grows from a tiny holdfast and then repeatedly divides. At the end of each branch is a swollen 'receptacle' where sex cells are produced. These receptacles are inflated, and when slightly dry, pop and explode under foot—a popular pastime for some younger beachcombers.

OTHER NAME: Bladder Wrack; Popping Wrack

RANGE: Southern California to Alaska

ZONE: middle intertidal

HABITATS: rocky shores

LENGTH: to 20 in

COLOR: olive-green, yellowish-green

Walking over rocks covered in this seaweed is hazardous—it produces slimy mucus to keep itself from drying out, but the mucus is devilishly slippery. Be sure to lift up the dangling fronds when beachcombing: it is very moist underneath and all kinds of organisms will be taking refuge here while the tide is out. A common twisting version of Rockweed is *Fucus spiralis*, and a diminutive form is called Little Rockweed (*Pelvetiopsis limitata*).

Tar Spot
RALFSIA PACIFICA

It's hard to believe that these encrusting dark brown or black spots are another species of brown alga—they are so easy to step over and ignore. They form thin, encrusting growths on rocks of the middle to lower intertidal zone. Most Tar Spots take on a circular shape, gradually growing outwards. Close inspection of the surface might reveal tiny lines radiating from the central point, as well as concentric ridges. Even under a microscope, it is hard to believe that this organism is really an alga. It is composed of thin layers of cells and tiny threads, all packed in with a tough coat.

RANGE: Southern California to Alaska
ZONE: middle to lower intertidal
HABITATS: rocky shores
DIAMETER: to 8 in
COLOR: dark brown, black
SIMILAR SPECIES: Blobs of Tar (p. 202)

These algae are highly tolerant of extreme conditions. Their dark colors ensure that they absorb most of the sun's radiation, and they become very hot. A tough outer coating helps protect them. Other species of similar encrusting algae can be encountered in shades of red and brown. This one might easily be mistaken for the aftermath of an oil spill, but rest assured, this time it is an alga!

Sea Staghorn
CODIUM FRAGILE

This distinctive green alga is often seen perched on the top or sides of rocks. It is a very dark green, almost black, and the velvety texture feels more like a sponge. From a small holdfast, columnar branches grow, and these branches repeatedly divide in two, giving that antler-like quality. The branches are firm and rounded, standing upright when young. As they grow longer, they droop with their own weight. A dusting of white occurs on some branches.

RANGE: Southern California to Alaska

ZONE: middle to lower intertidal; shallow subtidal

HABITATS: rocky shores

LENGTH: to 16 in

COLOR: very dark green

On close inspection, you might notice the sea slug *Elysia hedgpethi* that lives on this alga. The green pigment (chlorophyll) that the sea slug swallows while eating the alga continues to photosynthesize for some time, perhaps offering sugary nutrition to the slug. The alga is highly nutritious, loaded with vitamins and iron. In Japan it is sugared and eaten as a delicacy, or used in soups and as a garnish. Loved in Japan, it is hated by the fisheries of the East Coast—shellfish bind to it readily, and then the alga breaks off in storms, losing the valuable crop to the sea.

Enteromorpha Green Algae

ENTEROMORPHA SPP.

Pools along the highest splash-line of the waves are not easy places to live in. Filled with rainwater one minute and engulfed in sea spray the next, they suffer the beating sun and freezing snowfalls, too. One group of algae, Enteromorpha Green Algae, thrives under these trying conditions, and does well enough that whole pools can be filled with their dazzling green tangles. Tubular strands of these algae can be seen along seepages in the cliffs, on mudflats and in estuaries—most often where fresh water and seawater mix.

OTHER NAME: Confetti

RANGE: Southern California to Alaska

ZONE: above high-tide line; spray or splash

HABITATS: spraypools; brackish-water seepages; estuaries; mudflats

LENGTH: to 10 in

COLOR: brilliant green, yellow-green

SIMILAR SPECIES: Sea Lettuce (p. 192)

The fragile strands often fill with bubbles of oxygen, making them float on the surface of the pools. Several forms of these algae occur, all bright green or yellow-green and with either long, thin tubes or flattened, wider strands. When they die, they lose the green chlorophyll pigments and turn a ghostly white. Found worldwide, many cultures eat these algae because they are highly nutritious. If you are tempted, be very cautious—these highly tolerant algae frequently grow in polluted water.

Sea Lettuce
ULVA LACTUCA

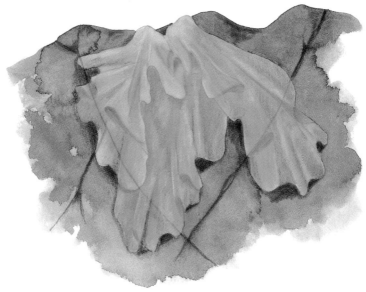

Bright green and frilled, this alga has earned the name 'Sea Lettuce.' It is edible and eaten as a rich source of vitamins and minerals in some parts of the world. The blades of the alga are only two cells thick, and are consequently translucent. When the oblong sheets dry out, they crinkle. Sea Lettuce attaches to rocks from the upper to lower intertidal zone, but is confined to tidepools in the upper zone. It can be seen gently drifting on mudflats and in estuaries, bays and lagoons.

There are several species of *Ulva*, or maybe not—biologists have yet to decide just how many we are dealing with. Some species come as uniform sheets, while others are perforated with holes and have tatty edges. Sea Lettuce turns up on other seaweeds, and occasionally attaches to the Pacific Plate Limpet (p. 59). If the water has gone green in a tidepool, this alga has released its tiny reproductive cells from the edges of its blades. Equally as green, Enteromorpha Green Algae grow as fine strands.

RANGE: Southern California to Alaska
ZONE: upper to lower intertidal
HABITATS: rocky shores; tidepools; calm waters
LENGTH: to 20 in
COLOR: bright green
SIMILAR SPECIES: Enteromorpha Green Algae (p. 191)

Nail Brush
ENDOCLADIA MURICATA

This very common alga has predominantly red pigments and appears dark red to purple, sometimes brown. It favors the very high reaches of the shore, where it clings to the rocks in the close company of hardy Acorn Barnacles (p. 155). Here, it is exposed to the rigors of intertidal life, drying up in hot sunshine. As it dries out, the colors become very dark, almost black, and the thin branches shrivel. When wet it is soft and supple, but when dry it is coarse and wiry. These are hardy tufts of algae, some of which might not feel the spray of the ocean for more than a day, because they grow so high in the intertidal zone.

OTHER NAME: Sea Moss
RANGE: Southern California to Alaska
ZONE: upper intertidal
HABITATS: rocky shores
LENGTH: to 3 in
COLOR: dark red, purple, black

Little clumps, resembling woodland moss, scatter the rocks of exposed and partially protected shores. The fine texture is made from many slender branches, each of which is covered by tiny spines. These dense little forests are well worth poking into, because many tiny creatures crawl inside the tangle to take shelter from predators and the elements.

Turkish Towel

GIGARTINA EXASPERATA

Turkish Towels are an attractive addition to rocky and cobble shores, where their splashes of red add to the browns and greens in the mats of seaweed. When very young its color is intense and bright, but as it ages, the seaweed becomes a very dark purple-red, losing its brilliance, and sometimes appearing almost black. The blades are long and wide, and covered in small nodules that give it a rough texture like a coarse towel. When submerged or very wet, the blades have an iridescent bluish sheen.

Several species of *Gigartina* grow from California all the way up to Alaska. They are only obvious in summer when the blades rapidly expand from small growths on the holdfast. In winter the blades die off and are a frequent addition to the wrack on the beaches after a storm. The little holdfast sits tight through winter, waiting for spring and new growth. Turkish Towels are an excellent source of carrageenan, an agent that is used in industry and foods for so many different applications.

RANGE: Southern California to British Columbia

ZONE: lower intertidal; subtidal to 60 ft

HABITATS: rocky shores; cobble shores

LENGTH: to 18 in

WIDTH: to 10 in

COLOR: bright red to very dark purple-red

Black Pine

RHODOMELA LARIX

Almost black when dry, this alga is rich brown when wet. It thrives on protected, rocky shores from the middle to lower intertidal zone, and is found on rocks or in tidepools. It gets its name from the short, needle-like clusters of branches coming off the main stem, or stipe. These clusters are spirally arranged around the cylindrical stipe. The growth habit of these needles resembles the larch tree, whose genus name, *Larix*, is the inspiration for the scientific name of this member of the red algae family.

In winter Black Pine's 'needles' drop off, leaving bare stems, but the stipes will grow back next spring. Several stipes will grow from one small hold-fast. Sometimes attached to the dense growth is the brown alga *Soranthera ulvoidea*. This alga is easily recognizable when it is mature, because it forms a large, bulbous growth almost 2 inches across. The dense growth of the Black Pine also makes an ideal hiding place for many small crustaceans. The Fir Needle (*Analipas japonicus*) is a similar seaweed, but is more thinned-out and has flatter 'needles.'

RANGE: Central California to Alaska
ZONE: middle to lower intertidal
HABITATS: rocky shores; sheltered coasts
LENGTH: to 12 in
COLOR: dark brown, blackish

Sea Sac

HALOSACCION GLANDIFORME

The peculiar Sea Sac can be seen in distinctive clumps on rocky shores. Because of the pigments it uses to harness the sun's light, it belongs in the family of red algae. Just to confuse you, it more often appears olive-green and sometimes brownish, but if you look near the base, you might see some reddish tints. The clumps resemble bunches of fingers or sausages, and they often grow in a distinct band along rocky shores of exposed and sheltered coasts. This band occurs in the middle intertidal zone. Such a distinct band is a good example of intertidal zonation: each plant or animal is specifically tied to one part of the zone because of competition, predation or physical factors.

RANGE: Southern California to Alaska
ZONE: middle intertidal
HABITATS: rocky shores
LENGTH: to 6 in
COLOR: olive-green, brown, reddish

The bulbous sacs arise from a tiny holdfast and are usually filled with water. A bubble is often at the top of a sac, and is an accumulation of gases made during photosynthesis on bright days. If you give the sac a gentle squeeze, watch out for the tiny jets of water that are being forced out of small pores in the thin wall of the plant.

Iridescent Seaweed

IRIDAEA CORDATA

This beautiful seaweed comes in a deep red, which is overlaid with an iridescence that gives tints of purple, blue and green to the fleshy blade. A newcomer to this alga would be forgiven for thinking that the oily sheen was from the aftermath of an oil spill—this beautiful phenomenon is entirely the product of nature.

From a small holdfast comes one dominant blade with several smaller blades that are all slippery-smooth. The edges undulate and are often torn by the action of the waves. Very young blades are blue. In winter, they die back, just leaving the sturdy holdfast from which new blades will grow the following spring.

RANGE: Southern California to Alaska

ZONE: lower intertidal; shallow subtidal

HABITATS: rocky shores

LENGTH: to 36 in

COLOR: deep red, iridescent

Like the Turkish Towel (p. 194), this seaweed is loaded with carrageenan. Research is under way to establish profitable and practical ways to commercially grow this alga. Such research is important, because it might offer a way of growing the seaweed without having to rape and pillage the shores for it, and consequently damage the habitats for many other organisms.

Coralline Algae

CORALLINA SPP.

Carpets of Coralline Algae coat the bottom and sides of some tidepools. Where other seaweeds get chewed to bits, these tough ones are left alone; the tidepool residents just don't enjoy them. Although often feathery in appearance, these algae have a very tough texture that results from heavily calcified walls. Cells deposit so much lime (calcium carbonate) that early naturalists thought they were studying a type of coral animal and not a plant!

Bright pink to deep purple, the fronds are often edged in white. These jointed branches arise from a flat, encrusting growth spreading over the rock. Most of the alga is rigid, but at the joints there is less lime, so some flexibility is the result. This pliancy is an advantage when the rough surf crashes in. Many different species of Coralline Algae never grow to more than a few inches in length. When they die, they rapidly bleach white. While most Coralline Algae avoid being eaten because of their toughness, some Coralline Algae grow as encrustations that might be grazed by some snails and chitons.

RANGE: Southern California to Alaska

ZONE: lower intertidal; shallow subtidal

HABITATS: rocky shores; open coasts

LENGTH: to 4 in

COLOR: bright pink to dark purple

Encrusting Coral

LITHOTHAMNIUM PACIFICUM

Often overlooked, these pretty crusts are not strange rocks, but algae related to Coralline Algae (p. 198). Forming small patches of tough growths, Encrusting Coral might merge to create large colonies, overlapping and growing on top of one another. Usually pink, this alga also comes in deep purple, and the edges or nodules on its surface might be fringed in white. An encrusting resident of rocks, it will also grow on shells and is commonly seen near the low-tide line, especially in tide-pools.

Many patches have knobs on the surface and small, white dots might be evident. It is from these dots that microscopic spores emerge to start new encrustations. The crustiness of this alga is attributed to the heavy deposits of lime (calcium carbonate) that it extracts from seawater. Despite being so hard, it does fall prey to some

OTHER NAME: Pink Rock Crusts

RANGE: Southern California to British Columbia

ZONE: low-tide line; shallow subtidal

HABITATS: rocks; shells; tidepools

DIAMETER: variable to several inches

COLOR: white, pink, purple

mollusks. The White-cap Limpet (p. 53) lives on it, and is frequently overgrown with it, and the extravagantly marked Lined Chiton (p. 105) adheres to it, grazing slowly and adopting pinkish coloration to blend in with the alga.

Surf Grass
PHYLLOSPADIX SPP.

On rocky shores, huge beds of Surf Grass sway back and forth with the wash of waves. These vivid green leaves are not those of algae, but rather of flowering plants, just like some relatives on land. They have a root system, instead of a holdfast, and require sediment to sink their roots into. The leaves are long, slim and a brilliant green, and the flowers are nestled tightly against the stems. There are two common species of Surf Grass that are essentially similar.

RANGE: Southern California to Alaska

ZONE: middle to lower intertidal

HABITATS: rocky shores; open coasts

LENGTH: to 36 in

COLOR: green

SIMILAR SPECIES: Eelgrass (p. 201)

Surf Grass beds are excellent habitats to poke around in. A small isopod (*Idotea montereyensis*), resembling Vosnesensky's Isopod (p. 162), clings to the leaves and matches the green color. Shield-backed Kelp Crabs (p. 152) can be seen tenaciously grasping with their long legs, as the leaves sway back and forth. Thick beds of Surf Grass are a favored hiding place for some crabs at low tide. Sometimes, the vivid green color is masked by an excessive growth of a fuzzy, red alga, *Smithora naiadum*. Surf Grass resembles Eelgrass, but needs rocky, wave-swept coasts and not the calmer sandy waters that Eelgrass requires.

Eelgrass
ZOSTERA MARINA

Don some waders and be sure to gently walk through the extensive Eelgrass meadows of quiet bays. Eelgrass prefers water with a gentle flow, where some fresh water has mixed with the sea. Like Surf Grass, which it resembles, Eelgrass is a flowering plant. The green leaves are strap-like, with inconspicuous flowers tucked near the stems. Eelgrass spreads through muddy sand with rooty rhizomes from which new plants grow.

The thick mat of Eelgrass stabilizes the soft mud, and is easy to walk on. The meadows are rewarding for the diverse wildlife they harbor. These are perfect nurseries for young fish and crabs, such as the Dungeness (p. 146) and Shield-backed Kelp Crabs (p. 152). Anemones wave their tentacles, while snails graze upon all kinds of encrustations and smother the leaves and stems. Nudibranchs creep about and pulsing jellyfish drift by. Shrimp dart around your feet. Clams have siphons peeking above the muddy surface and sea stars, including the massive Sunflower Star (p. 125), cruise along the bottom in search of prey. A meadow of Eelgrass is wildlife at your feet, and you don't have to watch out for dangerous waves!

RANGE: Southern California to Alaska

ZONE: lower intertidal, shallow subtidal

HABITATS: quiet bays; muddy bottom

LENGTH: to 36 in

COLOR: green

SIMILAR SPECIES: Surf Grass (p. 200)

Blobs of Tar

HOMINIS POLLUTANTISSIMUM

Beachcombing does come with minor hazards. Watch out for Blobs of Tar! These globular, black masses hide in sand, or stick to rocks. Try to avoid them if you can, because they are sticky and hard to remove. Get some on your skin and you will be scrubbing like crazy. Get some on your clothes and you might as well throw them away. Blobs of Tar can be tenacious and long lasting. Don't confuse them with the all-natural algal Tar Spots.

RANGE: Southern California to Alaska

ZONE: upper to lower intertidal; inshore; offshore

HABITATS: indiscriminate

LENGTH: microscopic to miles

COLOR: usually oily black

SIMILAR SPECIES: Tar Spot (p. 189)

Unfortunately, our beautiful oceans suffer from human activity in many ways. Blobs of Tar are tiny versions of larger problems—oil slicks. Tankers have accidents, and oil, in its various forms, pours onto the oceans, sticking to the feathers of birds and the soft fur of otters. These animals get waterlogged and die. Fish and shellfish suffocate, and many creatures are slowly poisoned. Oil is just one example of our neglect of the oceans. So remember that the oceans are sacred and think about your actions when you visit. Respect all wildlife and water, and please take all that garbage home with you.

Glossary

anal fin
the fin running underneath the fish behind the anus, but in front of the tail

aperture
the opening to the shell of gastropods out of which the animal emerges

bivalve
group of mollusks possessing two valves or shells that enclose the animal

byssal threads
tough threads made of strong protein secreted by some bivalves to attach themselves firmly to rocks

calcareous
whitish deposits or material made from calcium carbonate (lime), like shells

calcium carbonate
white, hard compound extracted from the sea to make shells, also called lime.

carapace
large, flat portion of the crab's shell covering the head and thorax from which the legs arise; often washed ashore after molting

carnivore
consumes other animals or parts of them

cerata
fleshy growths on the back of some nudibranchs, usually with an extension of the gut running inside

cirrus
hand-like appendages, or small, hairy growths; used in reference to growths on fish heads and the feathery feet of barnacles for filter feeding

commensal
where one organism lives with, in or on another, gaining some advantages such as food or shelter, without harming its host

GLOSSARY

crustacean
group of arthropods, including the crabs, shrimp and beach fleas

encrustation
usually a low, flat, firm growth (crust) covering a surface

estuarine
where a fresh water river exits into the sea; salinity drops because the salts are diluted by the fresh water, and both sea and river influence local geography

filter feeder
an organism that feeds using feathered or net-like appendages, or other means, to extract tiny or even microscopic particles suspended in the water

gastropod
molluskan snails, such as whelks, dogwinkles and limpets

girdle
fleshy band surrounding the plates of chitons

herbivore
consumes plants or parts of plants

holdfast
root-like structure with which seaweeds attach themselves to rocky substrates

intertidal zone
zone between low-tide line and high-tide line

mantle
sheet of living tissue that secretes the shells of snails and encloses the delicate gills

midrib
central rib running the length of some blades of kelp (absent in other species)

nematocyst
specialized stinging cells found in the tentacles of jellyfish, anemones and corals

nocturnal
active by night

nudibranch
another name for sea slug

omnivore
consumes pretty much anything it wants to, provided it is worth it

operculum
a horny door with which a gastropod shuts itself in; used to protect against predators, and to prevent from drying out during low tide

periostracum
tough organic layer on the shell of mollusks

plankton
tiny organisms suspended in water drifting at the mercy of the currents and tides

radula
tooth-like structure used for scraping or boring, taking on various forms depending on the diet of the gastropod or chiton

red tide
occasional blooms of a single-celled organism causes reddening of water; toxins from these organisms build up in the flesh of shellfish; not a toxin you want to consume

rhinophores
sensory structures, like tentacles, on the head of nudibranchs

salinity
level of salt in water; high salinity means lots of sea salt

sessile
sitting, or fixed, usually incapable of moving around, as in the case of barnacles and mussels

silica
hard mineral, like quartz and glass, occurring in sponge spicules

siphons
tube-like extensions from mollusks to obtain water that is drawn into the mantle cavity; particularly evident in burrowing bivalves

stipe
seaweed equivalent of a stem

test
tough supporting structure, or skeleton, of echinoderms, such as the Eccentric Sand Dollars found on beaches

umbo
located near the hinge of bivalve mollusks is the oldest part of the mollusk, often prominent and beak-like

valve
one half, or shell, of a bivalve

whorl
one complete turn of a spire on a snail shell

zooplankton
animal component of plankton (the plant element being phytoplankton)

zooid
individual member of a bryozoan colony

Further Reading

Behrens, David W. 1980. *Pacific Coast Nudibranchs*. Los Osos, California: Sea Challengers.

Delphine, Haley (ed). 1978. *Marine Mammals of the Eastern North Pacific and Arctic Waters*. Seattle, Washington: Pacific Search Press.

Eschmeyer, William, N. and Earl S. Herald. 1983. *Pacific Coast Fishes*. Peterson Field Guide Series. Boston, Massachusetts: Houghton Mifflin Company.

Goodson, Car. 1988. *Fishes of the Pacific Coast*. Stanford, California: Stanford University Press.

Gotshall, Daniel, W. 1994. *Guide to Marine Invertebrates: Alaska to Baja California*. Monterey, California: Sea Challengers.

Harbo, Rick M. 1997. *Shells and Shellfish of the Pacific Northwest*. Madeira Park, British Columbia: Harbour Publishing.

Jensen, Gregory C. 1995. *Pacific Coast Crabs and Shrimps*. Monterey, California: Sea Challengers.

Kozloff, Eugene, N. 1993. *Seashore Life of the Northern Pacific Coast: an illustrated guide to Northern California, Oregon, Washington and British Columbia*. Seattle, Washington: University of Washington Press.

Lamb, Andrew. 1986. *Coastal Fishes of the Pacific Northwest*. Madeira Park, British Columbia: Harbour Publishing.

Love, Milton. 1996. *Probably More Than You Want to Know About the Fishes of the Pacific Coast*. Santa Barbara, California: Really Big Press.

McConnaughey, B.H. and E. McConnaughey. 1988. *Pacific Coast*. The Audubon Society Nature Guides. New York: Alfred A. Knopf.

Morris, Percy, A. 1980. *Pacific Coast Shells*. Peterson Field Guide Series. Boston, Massachusetts: Houghton Mifflin Company.

Niesen, Thomas, M. 1997. *Beachcomber's Guide to Marine Life of the Pacific Northwest*. Houston, Texas: Gulf Publishing Company.

Paine, Stephanie Hewlett. 1992. *Beachwalker: Sea Life of the West Coast*. Vancouver/Toronto: Douglas & McIntyre.

Ricketts, Edward F. and Jack Calvin. 1968. *Between Pacific Tides*. Stanford, California: Stanford University Press.

Waaland, J. Robert. 1977. *Common Seaweeds of the Pacific Coast*. Seattle, Washington: Pacific Search Press.

Index

Page numbers in bold typeface indicate primary, illustrated species.

INDEX

INDEX

INDEX

INDEX

INDEX

About the Author

Ian Sheldon has lived in South Africa, Singapore, Britain and Canada. Caught collecting caterpillars at the age of three, he has been exposed to the beauty and diversity of nature ever since. He was educated at Cambridge University, England, and the University of Alberta, Canada. When he is not in the tropics working on conservation projects or immersing himself in our beautiful wilderness, he is sharing his love for nature. An accomplished artist, naturalist and educator, Ian enjoys communicating passion through the visual arts and the written word, in the hope that he will inspire love and affection for all nature.

Ian cavorts with a moonsnail at low tide.

MORE GREAT BOOKS ABOUT THE OUTDOORS